# Congratulations!

You just bought a book that keeps on giving.

Fifty percent of all proceeds from *Killing Wonder Woman* books
go to faith-based charities that help women win at their work
and/or soar in their faith.

To learn more about our giving partners,
visit: workingwomenoffaith.com/givingpartners

Thank you for changing the lives of women around the world
through your purchase!

## You rock!

TENAYA TJ TISON

# KILLING
# WONDER
# WOMAN

Setting Weary Women
Free to Win at Work
and Soar in Faith

WISE Ink
CREATIVE ★ PUBLISHING

ISBN 13: 978-1-63489-049-6

Library of Congress Catalog Number: 2016963142
Printed in the United States of America
First Printing: 2017
21   20   19   18   17          5   4   3   2   1


Cover Design: Chris Tobias, Tobias Outerwear for Books
Cover Artwork: Sarah K. Walker
Interior design: Dan Pitts

KILLING WONDER WOMAN ™ is a trademark of Tenaya Tison
All other trademarks and copyrights, referenced herein, are the property of their respective owners.

837 Glenwood Avenue
Minneapolis, MN 55405
wiseinkpub.com

To order visit: www.workingwomenoffaith.com/killingwonderwoman

# PRAISE FOR KILLING WONDER WOMAN

"T.J. Tison creates a compelling reason why your Wonder Woman needs to die. A great read with real insights and actionable ideas, coaching you how to live a more adventurous life God's way. Full of compelling real-life narratives, impactful insights, and revealing anecdotes to encourage the reader to be set free and allow God to use them more fully for His glory in the marketplace."

**—Kathryn M. Tack, executive coach, speaker, and trainer with the John Maxwell Team**

"*Killing Wonder Woman* equips you with the power of YOUR voice and gives you the choice to no longer shape your voice according to what you hear in the media, at work, at home, or from any other place. T.J.'s invitation to take this courageous journey is one of choice. You are given permission by God to set your Wonder Woman free and become the beautiful woman He has called you to be. A life-changing experience awaits you."

**—Suzann Brown, senior vice president, the Private Client Reserve of US Bank**

"My heart is filled with unspeakable joy because Tenaya (T.J.) Tison, a woman of power (*dunamis*), has enlightened us with truth to recognize the wiles of the enemy. The myth and disguise of Wonder Woman has depleted us long enough; the spiritual insight provided within this book will prepare every woman for battle, as she annihilates her enemies in aim to become healed within the depths of her soul. For over two decades, I have been speaking into the hearts of a myriad of women, who lost themselves along the way as they focused on fulfilling their life roles and responsibilities to please others. As you digest each page of this book, I am confident that you will be strengthened and revived to experience a change of life."

**—DaVetta "Dee" Collins, founder and CEO of Dunamis Woman Enterprise, LLC**

"*Killing Wonder Woman* is a thought-provoking, inspiring book written with faith-filled words about the real-world experiences of working women. In her thoughtful, nonjudgmental style, T.J. Tison has captures some of the everyday challenges of women and engages us as readers to rethink God's purpose and our part in those experiences. She challenges us to reconsider the many Wonder Women myths and hear the Biblical messages in ways not always spoken in traditional times. Be ready by the end of her book to reflect on the wonders of our womanhood and be challenged to rethink one's purpose and passion for faith at work."

**—Cindy Leines, owner and founder, CEL Public Relations, Inc.**

# TABLE OF CONTENTS

# DEDICATION

This is for you, Dad.

# INTRODUCTION

Before I tell you what this book is about, let me tell you what it's not.

This is not a Christian feminist manifesto. Jesus Christ did more to set women free than I ever could. He wrote that book already. You will be set free if you read this, set free to be the woman God made you to be.

This is not a book about marriage or parenthood—there are plenty of those out there already. I guarantee if you apply the principles in this book, it will have a profound effect in every area of your life. You were a woman before you were any of those other things.

This book is about you:

A woman, first.

A woman, created in the image of God.

A woman, a daughter of the King.

A woman, destined to soar in faith.

Some of the things you read in here may rattle your cage and change your heart, mind, and thinking. They're meant to. This book is intentionally disruptive. Most of us are walking through life like tapped-out, stressed-out zombies. Our own ideals, our frantic lives, our societal pressures, and the lies and labels that go along with them are destroying us. We gave them permission. And it's time we put a stop to them.

This is a call to arms, ladies! A call to fight against those lies and labels. A call to fight for our own joy and peace. A call to kill Wonder Woman once and for all.

On the other side of this book, my prayer is that the real you will be free to live like she never has before.

That's a big promise, but I serve a big God. He can handle it, He's up for the challenge, and He welcomes it! "Bring it on," He says. "I'm tired of seeing my daughters tired and weary from trying to be something they're not. I want to see them set free. I want to see them soar."

And soar you will!

# PART ONE

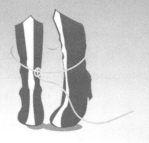

# KILLING
# WONDER
# WOMAN

Are you ready?

You are about to embark on a journey, an adventure—one filled with murder, deception, freedom, battle, and victory. It is an adventure fraught with danger, yet filled with promise. Promise of a life lived to the fullest. It is an adventure that all women of faith need to take to truly live.

You don't need to be brave, strong, or capable to go on this adventure. You only need to be willing. It is an adventure of choice.

The choice is yours.

You can choose to stay where you are now: frustrated, weary, overwhelmed, and living a "less-than" life. A life filled with defeat and discouragement.

Or, you can take a step forward, turn the page, and trust that God will be with you during every step of this adventure. Believe that this adventure is part of His heart for you. Part of His grand design for you to live the abundant life He promised.

Are you ready? Are you ready to kill Wonder Woman and finally set yourself free?

Turn the page and let's go!

# CHAPTER ONE

# WHO IS WONDER WOMAN?

The first rule of warfare is knowing your enemy. I wish I could tell you I know this enemy of mine well. Even though I have been fighting her my entire life, I only recently gave her a name. When I say recently, I mean six months ago when I got the idea for the title of this book. Before that, she was a nameless, faceless enemy who had been trying to ruin my life.

Naming this enemy sent me on a journey of looking back at battles from the past and the scars left behind as reminders. My reflections revealed an enemy who has been successful in attacking most women I know. We all bear the marks of battles lost and won. She has taken some of us out of the game, lied to us, cheated us, and wounded us greatly. She doesn't want us to name her. Naming her, and her lies and labels, gives us the power to defeat her.

I have a confession to make. I'm not some buff veteran warrior who is deft at wielding weapons, winning every battle. I'm not a killing machine. I'm just an ordinary girl with an extraordinary God.

I came from a middle-class family, grew up in upper middle-America, and had a middle-of-the-road childhood (some good, some bad). There is nothing that special about my life story that qualifies me as an expert in killing Wonder Woman. Any one of you could have written this book too. You have also been fighting this enemy your whole life—you just didn't realize it, and you just haven't named her yet. That all ends right here. Her name is Wonder Woman, and we are going to kill her together.

If we are going to kill Wonder Woman, we must first understand who she is.

> **Wonder Woman is any ideal, label, or lie you feel compelled to live up to and use in order to define and measure yourself and your worth.**

Some of these ideals and labels may not be inherently bad on their own. But too often we allow them to become what defines us, a measure of our worth, taking control of our lives. They turn into soul-crushing, life-draining, heart-breaking impediments to living the life God intended for us.

When was the first time you felt like you weren't good enough? Was it when a parent compared you to a sibling? "Why can't you be more like your sister/brother?" Was it when a teacher announced, "The whole class needs to be more like so-and-so." Was it when you saw that beautiful woman on the cover of some magazine or watched a movie star on the big screen? Think back. When was that first moment you unwittingly let Wonder Woman into your life? When did you first put some ideal of a woman on a pedestal and start trying to emulate someone you're not?

I found my first Wonder Woman in ballet class. I loved everything about ballerinas as a little girl. They were graceful and slender. They floated almost on air to the music and performed physical feats with ease. One little ballerina in my class became my first Wonder Woman. Her name was Jessica. Everything about her composed a beautiful ballerina, and I immediately measured myself against her. She had flawless posture; I slouched. She had a ballerina body; I had a pooching stomach and thick thighs. She could do pirouettes with precision; I often lost my balance and stumbled. If only I could be like Jessica! Then I could be a great ballerina.

This was only the first of many Wonder Women I let into my life. Who was your first Wonder Woman?

If you can't think of one yet, you will by the end of this chapter. Wonder Woman is sneaky. She isn't going to stand up, wave her arms wildly, and say, "Here I am!" She's incognito because she knows if you spot her and deal with her, she's doomed. You're going to need some help finding her.

I divided Wonder Woman into her three usual disguises: Mythical, Spiritual, and Actual. You may recognize one or all of these in your life. You may have only a few, but I'm willing to guess you have many. When you begin to recognize Wonder Woman in your life and expose her for what she is, you'll be better equipped to kill her.

## Mythical Wonder Woman

The Mythical Wonder Woman is the "not real life" woman we attempt to imitate. She is the fictional persona introduced to us through books, television, and movies. We want to be like her; we wish we were her. We try to emulate her in hopes that our lives will turn out to be more like hers and less like ours. The Wonder Woman of comics, TV, and movies is one of them.

The comic book Wonder Woman was the creation of a man named Dr. William Moulton Mauston. Mauston was a polygamist, feminist, and psychologist (yeah, that explains a lot, doesn't it?). His reason for developing her? Mauston confessed, "Frankly, Wonder Woman is psychological propaganda for the new type of woman who, I believe, should rule the world."[1] Wonder Woman had incredible strength and power. She was cool and confident. She had an awesome invisible jet, could deflect bullets, and used a lasso of truth so people could not lie to her (who doesn't want one of those?). She defeated evil and waged war for justice. Just the kind of woman World War II America needed at the time (Mauston had some other twisted ideas behind her character, but we won't go into those here).

This comic was eventually adapted into a TV show in the 1970s (which, ironically, was on the TV the first night I was writing this book. Hmmm, coincidence? I think not).

I remember watching this show as a little girl. I remember wishing I was Wonder Woman. Lynda Carter, who played the female superhero, had piercing blue eyes, a tiny waist, long legs, and a cute button nose. I had none of the above. In fact, I was the opposite of TV Wonder Woman. I wasn't brave and strong, or able to defeat evil. I was scared and weak. If only I could be like Wonder Woman! Then, I could fight the evil that permeated my young life and overcome all my enemies.

I was sexually abused when I was eleven. The abuse lasted for a couple years and left scars that have faded, but will always remain. Unfortunately, many of you can relate to that senseless trauma. I remember thinking as a little girl that if I were strong enough and brave enough, I could've stopped him. If I were like Wonder Woman, he wouldn't have messed with me.

There were other fictional Wonder Women in my younger years: Dorothy from the Wizard of Oz, Nancy Drew, Pippi Longstocking, Anne of Green Gables, Scarlet O'Hara, and Princess Leia. Not to mention all the Disney princesses like Snow White, Sleeping Beauty, and Cinderella. Today, not much has changed. Our little girls emulate Katniss, Hermione, Ariel, Jasmine, Elsa, Dora, etc.

The crazy thing is, the Mythical Wonder Woman isn't even real. She is a fictional character on the pages of literature, and on TV and movie screens, but she isn't real. She is the figment of someone's imagination. Yet, how many of us spent our formative years admiring and aspiring to be like these mythical Wonder Women? No wonder we feel so woefully inadequate and insufficient in our own lives! We've spent years looking up to people who do not even exist, or perhaps existed in some form of history, but were delivered to us through a shiny, filtered lens.

Mythical Wonder Woman is a make-believe lie designed to make some company, author, or franchise a ton of money. And we have bought into her hook, line, and sinker. Our bookshelves, DVD cases, and Netflix queues lay filled with lies that we paid for with our hard-earned money. We not only bought the lies, but we gave them entrance into our hearts and minds. We've come to believe the lie that if we are smart enough, pretty enough, strong enough, or brave enough, then we too can live happily ever after, just like all the books we read and movies we watched. Every Disney movie I can think of had a happy ending. Disney lied to us! Actually, Wonder Woman used Disney (and the like) to lie to us.

Some of these mythical Wonder Women have character traits that are admirable. Strength, justice, love, courage, individuality—these traits drew us to them. What trapped us in their snare was believing the lie that these women were a measure of our own personal worth and that emulating them would bring us happiness and fulfillment.

I am not advocating we never read a book or watch a movie again. But when we do, we'd better do it with eyes wide open and hearts and minds guarded. Admire the good and call out the lies. Refuse to give Mythical Wonder Woman an inch of your worth. If you give her an inch, she will take a mile (and much more!) from you in return.

 **Let's be honest:** ★ ★

*Can you see her? Can you see your Mythical Wonder Woman (or women)?*
*Who is she? Which fictional Mythical Wonder Woman did you set up in*
*your life as something to attain?*
*What was it about her that made you want to be like her?*
*How did you measure up?*
*What lies have you believed from your Mythical Wonder Woman?*

## Spiritual Wonder Woman

There's another Wonder Woman in our lives. One more insidious and damaging than the mythical one. She's the one who deceives us the most because her lies have a basis in truth, at least in part.

Spiritual Wonder Woman is: the biblical or spiritual characters or truths that have been spoon-fed into our hearts as a measure of our worth. She is displayed as an example in practice, when she is actually an example in principle. She is forever telling us that we are not good enough.

Let's take the woman in Proverbs 31, for example. No Bible character or persona has been more twisted in pursuit of holiness than this one. There are conferences and retreats surrounding the Proverbs 31 woman. There are organizations formed upon her, books written about her, and promises made to be more like her. She is even called a Spiritual Wonder Woman by many in the faith community. If you have never read about this superhero of women, here is the passage that describes her:

*Who can find a virtuous and capable wife?*
*She is more precious than rubies.*
*Her husband can trust her,*
*and she will greatly enrich his life.*

*She brings him good, not harm,*
*all the days of her life.*

*She finds wool and flax*
*and busily spins it.*
*She is like a merchant's ship,*
*bringing her food from afar.*
*She gets up before dawn to prepare breakfast for her household*
*and plan the day's work for her servant girls.*

*She goes to inspect a field and buys it;*
*with her earnings she plants a vineyard.*
*She is energetic and strong,*
*a hard worker.*
*She makes sure her dealings are profitable;*
*her lamp burns late into the night.*

*Her hands are busy spinning thread,*
*her fingers twisting fiber.*
*She extends a helping hand to the poor*
*and opens her arms to the needy.*
*She has no fear of winter for her household,*
*for everyone has warm clothes.*

*She makes her own bedspreads.*
*She dresses in fine linen and purple gowns.*
*Her husband is well known at the city gates,*
*where he sits with the other civic leaders.*
*She makes belted linen garments*
*and sashes to sell to the merchants.*

*She is clothed with strength and dignity,*
*and she laughs without fear of the future.*
*When she speaks, her words are wise,*
*and she gives instructions with kindness.*

*She carefully watches everything in her household*
*and suffers nothing from laziness.*

*Her children stand and bless her.*
*Her husband praises her:*
*"There are many virtuous and capable women in the world,*
*but you surpass them all!"*

*Charm is deceptive, and beauty does not last;*
*but a woman who fears the LORD will be greatly praised.*
*Reward her for all she has done.*
*Let her deeds publicly declare her praise.*

(Prov 31: 10–30 [New International Version])

Just reading through this passage again causes my anxiety of inadequacy to soar to new levels. I can't even relate to this woman, let alone be like her. I have no idea how to spin wool; I can't sew; I don't get up to make breakfast for everyone; I don't have servant girls (except in my dreams); I bring my food from aclose, not afar. The woman described here is perfect in every way, and I'm doomed to fail before I even start.

Many scholars debate if this was an actual woman or the picture of the ideal wife a mother wanted for her son. I'm not here to declare one way or the other, but many women have tripped over this Spiritual Wonder Woman, including me.

Too many within the church use the Proverbs 31 woman to define what a God-fearing woman looks and acts like. Some have even used her as a type of permission for husbands to exert demands upon their wives. Such scripture-twisting practices are a tool used by the Spiritual Wonder Woman. The result is that women believe the lie that if they aren't just like her, they aren't godly women. She is lifted up as the standard for all women, the example to follow, the one to measure yourself against. If you don't measure up, you have a lot of work to do.

There are some sound principles behind this picture of a woman, but her practices are impossible to meet.

Think about other Bible characters like Mary, Deborah, or the widow with two mites (Lk 21:1–4).

I can never be like the Virgin Mary. I am not a virgin, and I don't live in Israel at the time the Messiah was to be born. But I can follow her example of surrendering to the will of God, even when it doesn't make sense to me.

I can never be like Deborah. I am not a judge, and I don't know how to fight in a battle. But I can follow her example of bravery in the face of an enemy.

I can never be like the widow with two mites because I'm not a widow, and I don't have mites. But I can follow her example of giving my resources to God.

We can follow this line of reasoning with these biblical characters, but when it comes to the Proverbs 31 woman, we believe we need to live out her daily practice.

There's nothing wrong with admiring the character and accomplishments of these godly women. Just don't measure your success in your faith journey, or your worth to God, against them. Why not? Because you aren't them and you never will be. If God wanted you to be Esther, He would've made you Esther. But He made you who you are because He loves you that way.

Maybe the Proverbs 31 woman isn't your Spiritual Wonder Woman. Maybe it's a male biblical character or a spiritual truth that was twisted before it was given to you—one you grew up believing because that's all you knew. You never questioned it or compared it to God's truth.

The Spiritual Wonder Woman is just another label and another lie. A dangerous one at that. Spiritual Wonder Woman is the most dangerous of all because it plays on our desire to please God. It's the lie that if I just do this, or don't do that, then God will love me more.

The lie of the Spiritual Wonder Woman is: God doesn't love us as we are and will only accept us if we are like someone else. That's a lie we can no longer afford to believe. It's robbing us of an abundant, full life and we need to say, "Enough!"

  **Let's be honest:**

*Do you have a Spiritual Wonder Woman? Who is she?*
*How did she become your Spiritual Wonder Woman?*
*What would it take to be like her?*
*What lies have you believed from your Spiritual Wonder Woman?*
*Have you ever felt guilty or ashamed because you didn't live up to her example?*

## Actual Wonder Woman

The Actual Wonder Woman is real and present, where our other Wonder Women were fictional and past. She does a lot of damage without us even noticing. She is a duplicitous creature because she comes in many forms.

1.  She is your mother, your grandmother, your sister, your friend, or your neighbor down the street. She is a real, live woman you are always comparing yourself to or trying to imitate. She's the one who is a phenomenal cook, when you burn everything. She is a size six after having four kids, while you are trying to squeeze into your size eighteen jeans. She is kind to everyone, while you lash out at those you love most. She has a nice husband/kids/house/whatever, and you lack on every side. She seems to have it all together, while you seem to be falling apart at the seams. You call her a Wonder Woman, a Superwoman, even if only in your mind. You are certain if

she can do it, you can do it too. So you try with all your might and still don't measure up.

2. She is the messages from your culture, your family, and the media. The messages that tell you who you are, who you should be, or who you could be if you only tried harder. That celebrity or model who is a complete package of beauty and success. That cultural expectation thrust upon you without your permission. That family member who is better than the rest and makes us question how the gene pool skipped over us. Messages that scream, "You are less than these!"

3. She is that co-worker or colleague who is smarter and more accomplished than you. That speaker at the conference who has such a way with words. That woman at church who is gifted in all the areas you wish you were. Pictures of success in work and faith. Ideal women who managed to make themselves into something. Yet here you are in a dead-end job, feeling like you have nothing to offer the world, or God, for that matter.

4. She is yourself. Your self-imposed idea of what a fulfilled, successful, and happy life looks like. That picture-perfect life you created and dreamed of as a girl, or picked up somewhere along the way. The one you don't have right now. The one that will bring you happiness if only you could grasp it.

When I was eighteen, I mapped out what my life would look like. I would wait to get married until I was twenty-six, I wouldn't have kids until I was thirty. I would marry my high school sweetheart and we would have three kids. I would have a fulfilling teaching career and live in a big city.

How did that vision turn out? I got married when I was twenty (not to my high school sweetheart either, thank God!). I had two kids, my first at twenty-two. I have a fulfilling career in business (but not until recently). My husband and I live on a farm in Wisconsin . . .

All pretty much the opposite of what I had "planned." I will say I'm sooo glad things didn't turn out like I thought they would, but many women view a different life plan as a failure because of the Actual Wonder Woman.

The Actual Wonder Woman, and her lies, gains access to us through our own insecurities. She diminishes our worth by showing us real women who accomplished what seems impossible. The impossible we think we want or need. The impossible we think will make us happy. But her lies are just that: lies.

You may not recognize her right away. You may have to dig beneath the surface to locate her deception. She may only appear in sound bites in your head now and then, but she is there. She chips away at your heart bit by bit. She whispers to you that if you were even a smidgen like this Actual Wonder Woman, you would be happy at last.

## ★ ★ Let's be honest: ★ ★

*Can you see her now?*
*Which of the four Actual Wonder Women do you see in your life?*
*How has this Wonder Woman lied to you?*

# Wonder Woman Shouts

These Wonder Women—Mythical, Spiritual, or Actual—become the voices in our choices. The only way to discover which Wonder Woman is speaking the loudest lies to you is to be silent and listen. Do you ever get a moment's peace?

A time to be silent and still? To hear the quietness of a second in time?

It's rare in our busy lives to find such a gem, but if you do, what do you hear? Do you hear the stillness of the moment, or do your thoughts begin to pour in at a rapid pace? What do your thoughts tell you in that space in time when your earth stands still for a nanosecond? What voices do you hear? Which voices speak the loudest?

Chances are pretty good that your voices start a litany of accusations against you—all the ways you don't measure up to your Wonder Women. All your broken promises and failed attempts of trying to be like her.

There are a million Wonder Women voices speaking to us every day. Not just speaking, but shouting. Yelling and telling us who we are and how we just don't measure up. Not all voices in our lives are looking out for our best interests. In fact, most of the voices in our lives have their own agenda. These Wonder Woman voices never seem to stop talking:

- The voice of the news media and parent mania
- The voice of your society and your workplace
- The voice of your family and your faith
- The voice of your successes and your failures
- The voice of past woes and future worries
- The voice of your friends and your foes

Every voice of Wonder Woman that we allow into our ears, hearts, and minds feeds our beliefs on some level. True or not, these beliefs color our choices and persuade our actions. Whose voice are you listening to today?

If you listen to the voices that speak life and peace, your choices will follow.

If you listen to voices that speak hate and shame, your choices will follow.

Which voice are you listening to? It will determine your choices.

There is a better way. There is a true voice of love and forgiveness that can drown out every other voice you hear.

In the midst of the cacophony of Wonder Women voices is the voice of the One whispering how He loves you more and knows you better than anyone else. That is the voice of God. When you choose to believe in God's Son, Jesus, and what He has done for you, you will start to hear the Voice of Truth over the Wonder Woman lies. When you choose to listen to that voice of love and grace, you will be able to spot Wonder Woman's lies from a mile away. Your life will take on new meaning, and your actions will show it.

Here's a list of what THAT voice says about you, the voice of a God who loves you and longs for you to hear His whispers of love over Wonder Woman's shouts.

God says, as His daughter, you are:

- His possession

- His workmanship

- His friend

- His temple

- His vessel

- His co-laborer

- His witness


When you are quiet and still, you will hear God's voice saying you are:

- A soldier

- An ambassador

- A building

- A minister

- An instrument

- A saint


In that moment of stillness, let God whisper to you that you have been:

- Redeemed

- Forgiven

- Set free from sin

- Set free from satan

- Set free from the kingdom of darkness

- Chosen before the foundation of the world

- Predestined to be like Jesus

- Forgiven of all your trespasses

- Given a sound mind

- Given the Holy Spirit

- Adopted into God's family

- Given great and precious promises

If you chose to believe THAT voice over all the voices of Wonder Woman filling your head, how different would your life be? How would you look at yourself if you silenced your Wonder Women and listened to God instead?

It's not just about the voices we hear, but which ones we choose to believe that determine our choices and actions.

## Let's be honest:

*Can you sit still in quietness for the next five minutes?*
*Whose voice is speaking the loudest? Wonder Woman's? Or God's?*
*How much energy do you spend trying to be like her?*

# CHAPTER TWO

# WHY KILL WONDER WOMAN?

After seeing the wreckage that Wonder Woman causes in our hearts, minds, and lives, I hope I won't have to spend too much time convincing you to kill her. If you don't kill Wonder Woman, she will kill you.

I'm going to let you in on a little secret, and if you get one thing from this book, get this:

Wonder Woman and satan are in cahoots.

That's right. They have teamed up to feed you a lifetime of lies and labels to render you ineffective and paralyzed in your faith and life.

Look back at your Wonder Women in the categories discussed in the previous chapter. Think about the lies and labels that go along with each one you discovered and how they have worn you down. I don't know about you, but that makes me tired.

Tired of seeing women hemmed in by labels and paralyzed by lies.

Tired of seeing women who are weary and worn out from trying to live up to these ideals.

Are you weary? When is the last time you didn't collapse into bed at night? Do you struggle to keep your eyes open past 8:00 p.m.

because you've spent your whole day and all your limited energy trying to live an impossible life?

I'm weary, and I'm mad. And you should be mad too.

Think about what your heart and life would be like if it weren't for Wonder Woman and satan and all the damage they have caused. Does it make you mad? Are you angry that you have been duped by the great deceiver for all these years?

I'm mad that it's cost me years of joy.

I'm at a point in my "seasoned" age where I don't give as much space to Wonder Woman as I did when I was younger. I don't have the patience for her antics anymore. I realize how much time, energy, and money I wasted listening to her. I remember making myself crazy trying to live up to her ideals. I used to be a bit fanatical about how my house looked, how my kids were dressed, and how "put together" I appeared to everyone around me. I spent a lot of years forfeiting my joy in exchange for her empty lies. That makes me really mad!

And I'm mad that we aren't doing anything to stop it. We have all let her steal our joy and waste precious time and energy. When will we stop her? When will we stop the madness of living up to some ideal Wonder Woman that society, and even the faith community, has defined for us? We just sit back and take whatever lies are spoon-fed to us.

Hillary Clinton tells us in one of her books to make Hard Choices.[2] Sheryl Sandberg's book tells us to Lean In[3]. Everyone has an opinion of how women should live, love, and work. And none of them are helping us. Even the faith community has been silent on women and their careers. You can't swing a dead cat without hitting a book or article on how women can, or can't, have it all. And how to balance it once they get it.

It's time to put an end to the lies and labels that tell us who we should be and how we should live. It's time to declare war on Wonder Woman and her lies, and replace it with Truth.

God didn't create us to live in some mold defined by others. He created us to be free, live abundantly, and walk beautifully and uniquely in the purpose He created for us before we were even born.

We need to kill Wonder Woman because she deserves to die. She has stolen precious time and heart space from us, and she needs to be stopped.

We need to kill Wonder Woman because she is holding us captive, holding us back, and holding us down from soaring in our faith as God intended.

We need to kill Wonder Woman because, unless and until we do, she will keep destroying us and every generation to follow.

## Wonder Woman Holds You Captive

Have you ever told a lie? Have you ever noticed how that lie holds you captive? Once told, you are now beholden to that lie to keep it alive. It is the lies we choose to believe that also hold us captive.

Wonder Woman and satan have been lying to you your entire life. If you don't kill her, you will remain captive to her lies. Did you know that scripture calls satan the Father of Lies? He is the originator of the lie and a master of it as well. The best liar you know doesn't even come close to satan's abilities in the lie arena.

He even takes truth and twists it, or leaves a part of it out, to pass a lie off as truth. He did it with Jesus in the wilderness; he'll do it to you as well. You see this truth-twisting pretty clearly when looking at your Spiritual Wonder Woman.

Wonder Woman and satan like to tell us the same lies over and over again. This kind of lie reinforcement keeps us bound and captive to the lies. We are bound in chains of deceit and we don't even realize it.

We aren't just told lies about who we are, we are told lies about who God is.

Lies like:

- •God couldn't love me after what I've done
- •God only loves good people
- •God is angry with me
- •God doesn't have a plan for my life
- •God doesn't answer my prayers

We may not voice those lies out loud for fear of heresy, but our faith and our actions speak otherwise. There was a space of about ten years in my life when I didn't follow God. I turned from the truth I had known because I listened to Wonder Woman lies instead of the truth of my loving Father. At the end of those ten years, I had veered so far from my precious faith that I didn't even recognize myself anymore. I was weary and miserable. I ended up separated and headed for divorce because of my detour.

It was hard for me to return to God in that state because I believed the lie that He couldn't love me after what I had done. Thankfully, God's forgiveness is bigger than my mistakes. God did forgive me. He performed a miracle in my heart and in our marriage and we just celebrated twenty-five years together! If I would have continued to believe the lies, you wouldn't be reading this right now. We go through life believing the lies dished up and served to us (like I did), and wonder why we are so weary and miserable.

The only way to break free from the captivity of the lies is to kill Wonder Woman.

## Wonder Woman Holds You Back

In addition to all the lies with which satan and Wonder Woman hold us captive, they also use labels to hold us back.

Labels are general descriptions of contents. Pick up any canned good from your pantry. The label tells you what is in the can, but does not give detailed amounts for every ingredient. Labels put people in a bucket or category. They make it easy for us to control and navigate our knowledge about people and situations.

Labels are limiting.

You've most likely heard the phrase, "Don't put God in a box." Meaning, don't limit God to your knowledge and understanding. Shouldn't the same be true of us? We were divinely and uniquely created. A loving, heavenly Father crafted us for an exact and specific purpose before He created the world.

You are made in the image of God.

I am made in the image of God.

Each person on the earth is made in the image of God.

Think about that. God. Perfect. Holy. Infallible. And He chose to make us—you—in the image, likeness of Himself. God gave us a great gift, and imparted great value upon us, when He made us in His image.

When we buy into these labels, and demean and belittle ourselves or others, are we not, in essence, insulting our God?

God thought you were precious enough to make you in the likeness of Himself. You are special and unique by design. You are one-of-a-kind. Although we are all made in the image of God, we are all made uniquely for God's glory and His purposes.

The labels of Wonder Woman hold us back from that unique design and purpose. We start to believe we're nothing special, and nothing could be further from the truth. Wonder Woman tells us to be like someone else, everyone else. To be happy. God tells us the opposite.

If we don't kill Wonder Woman and her labels, we will continue walking through life thinking and believing that we are nothing special. We will continue to think we need to be more like our Wonder Women.

When we try to be Wonder Woman—someone we're not—aren't we telling God that His creation of us is flawed?

Can you see the vicious cycle that holds us back?

# Wonder Woman Holds You Down

Think of what could happen if you killed Wonder Woman and her untruths. If you weren't held captive by lies and labels, you could actually soar in your faith.

Wonder Woman and satan don't want you to soar in your faith. They want to keep you grounded. They don't want you to be set free.

There's a story told by Chuck and Nancy Missler in their book *Faith in the Night Seasons* that goes like this:

A wounded eaglet was rescued by a kind farmer. He found the bird in one of his fields and so took him home, tended to his wounds and then placed him outside in the barnyard to recover.

Strangely enough, the young eaglet soon adapted to the habits of all the barnyard chickens. He learned to walk and cluck like them. He learned to drink from a trough and peck the dirt for food, and for many years he peacefully resigned himself to this new life on the ground.

But then one day, one of the farmer's friends spotted the eagle and asked, "Why in the world is that bird acting like a chicken?" The farmer explained what had happened. Even so, the man could hardly accept the situation.

"It's just not right," said the friend. "The Creator made that bird to soar in the heavens, not scavenge in the barnyard!" So he picked up the unsuspecting eagle, climbed onto a nearby fence post, and tossed him into the air. But the confused bird just fell back to earth and searched for his feathered friends.

Undaunted, the man then grabbed the eagle and climbed to the top of the barn. As he heaved him off the roof, the bird made a few halfhearted squawks and flaps before falling into a bale of hay.

After shaking his head a few times, the eagle then made himself comfortable and began mindlessly pecking at pieces of straw.

The friend went home that night dejected and could barely sleep as he remembered the sight of those powerful talons caked with barnyard mud. He couldn't bear the thought, so the very next day, he headed back to the farm for another try. This time he carried the eagle to the top of a nearby mountain where the sky unfolded in a limitless horizon.

He looked into the eagle's eyes and cried out, "Don't you understand? You weren't made to live like a chicken! Why would you want to stay down here when you were born for the sky?" As the man held the confused bird, he made sure the eagle was facing into the brilliant light of the setting sun. Then he powerfully heaved the bird into the sky, and this time the eagle opened his wings, looked at the sun, caught the updraft rising from the valley and disappeared into the clouds of heaven.[4]

As God's daughters, we were born to fly. We were created by a loving God to soar. He has called us to live in the heights, yet too many of us have huddled together in the barnyard and become content and comfortable with the crumbs that Wonder Woman gives us.

> **"One can never consent to creep**
> **when he feels an impulse to soar."**
> **–Helen Keller**

God's people need to cultivate and exercise that impulse. If we do, we will one day soar like eagles (Isa. 40:31 [New International Version]). We were meant to soar. Wonder Woman must be killed or we will continue to peck at the ground like chickens, never soaring on wings as eagles.

Do you see now why Wonder Woman must be killed? Hasn't she taken enough from you?

##  Let's be honest:

*List the lies of Wonder Woman that are holding you captive.*
*What labels of Wonder Woman have skewed your view of God's purpose*
*for your life?*
*Do you feel like you are soaring, or held down in your faith?*
*What has Wonder Woman stolen from you?*
*Are you mad enough about it to do something to stop her?*

# HOW TO KILL WONDER WOMAN

How exactly does one go about killing Wonder Woman? She's stronger than most of us, and has been around a lot longer. She is Wonder Woman, after all. How can mere mortals like you and me hope to defeat someone with super powers?

Thankfully, we know someone who is more powerful than Wonder Woman and all her lies and labels. Only God Almighty can help us defeat her. The key to unleashing God's power on our foe is to initiate the attack. When we step out in faith to kill Wonder Woman, God will step in to give us the power to complete the task.

When Jesus was preaching to a big crowd, the disciples told him to send the people away so they could eat, but Jesus said, "You feed them" (Mt. 14:15–21 [New Living Translation]). Jesus knew the disciples couldn't feed those masses without His power. Yet, He wanted them to take the first step.

Then there was the time Jesus sent seventy disciples out to preach the gospel (Lk 10). They went out and He gave them the power to heal the sick, blind, and lame, as well as cast out demons all on their own. They stepped forward to obey and, as they went, Jesus gave them the power to perform miracles.

Finally, when Moses was leading the people of Israel out of Egypt, God led them to a dead end. Trapped between the immense Red Sea on one side and the advancing Egyptian army on the other, it appeared this was the end. With all hope lost and death imminent, it looked as if disaster was certain.

What did Moses do in this situation? He told the people to wait, to stand still.

"But Moses told the people, 'Don't be afraid. Just stand still and watch the LORD rescue you today. The Egyptians you see today will never be seen again. The LORD himself will fight for you. Just stay calm'" (Ex. 14:13–14 [New Living Testament]).

We like to look at those verses out of context and use them for justification for our fears, faithlessness, and idleness. But the command to stand still came from Moses and his own fears, not from God.

Look at the next verse:

*"Then the LORD said to Moses, 'Why are you crying out to me? Tell the people to get moving!'"*

(Ex. 14:15 [New Living Testament]).

Moses' plan was to stand still; God's plan was to get moving. God had a miracle of biblical proportions up His sleeve, but He couldn't give that miracle to the people unless they moved.

God gave Moses His "next step," but it required action on Moses's part. What would have happened if Moses didn't move when God said move? Potentially, he and all the Israelites would have died. Or returned to a life of slavery in Egypt. There would have been no display of God's mighty power. No basis for epic movies showing the parting of the Red Sea.

No deliverance.

No promised land.

No victory.

So what could have kept Moses, and what keeps us, from "getting moving" when God says move? One thing: fear.

That same one thing will keep you from attacking and killing Wonder Woman and breaking free.

Fear of success (What happens after I kill her successfully? What then?).

Fear of failure (What if I don't kill her, but only maim her instead? Will I never find freedom?).

Fear is the opposite of faith.

•Fear freezes our fortitude.

•Fear stops us in our tracks.

•Fear tells us to keep standing still because it is safer than stepping out.

•Fear keeps us from seeing God's power.

•Fear prevents us from the Promised Land that God has for us.

We have to let our faith be bigger than our fears.

Moses did.

He got moving and obeyed God's "next step," which was to stretch his staff over the sea. It may not have looked like much of a "next step," but it was enough.

### God only needs a tiny speck of our faith to initiate His mighty power.

Stretching out his staff over the sea, Moses made a little movement of faith. A movement that didn't seem like anything momentous. Yet, it was enough for God to part an entire sea and dry up the ground underneath, providing a clear path forward. God didn't ask Moses to part the sea. God asked Moses to stretch out his hand in faith. He asked Moses to move.

### Taking a leap of faith starts
### with just one step.

I first had the idea to write this book four years ago. I stood paralyzed with fear because I didn't consider myself a writer. When I finally decided to move and told God I was ready, He performed a miracle. First, He had a friend offer me the free use of her lake cabin where I could go away and write the book (who wouldn't take someone up on that offer!?). When I went away to write it, I wrote it in only four days. Yes, you read that right. Four days! I told you it was miraculous. If I had stayed paralyzed with fear, I would have missed God's miracles and you wouldn't be killing Wonder Woman.

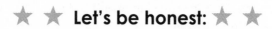

## ★ ★ Let's be honest: ★ ★

*Are you willing to take that step of faith to kill the*
*Wonder Women of your life?*
*What one fear is holding you back from killing her?*
*How will you fight that fear with faith?*

When you're ready to kill, say out loud, "I'm ready to kill Wonder Woman!"

Once you decide to take that step of faith and initiate God's power, these next three steps will help you kill Wonder Woman dead.

## Arm Yourself for Battle

Once you make the choice to pursue and kill Wonder Woman, you step onto the battleground. You see, Wonder Woman (a.k.a. satan) will not give up without a fight. She won't hand you over to freedom without trying to stop you.

In reality, you have been in the battle ever since you started your relationship with God and there has been an assault against your heart since the day you were born. An assault to keep you from coming to God. To keep you from having a personal relationship with Him through His Son, Jesus. To keep you from seeing and living His plan for your life. Once you come to God, there is another assault launched to lure you off that plan.

You are in the battle; you are at war. Up until now, you've just been sleeping through that war.

One of the greatest lies we face as believers is that there is no war going on. That spiritual warfare was only in Jesus's day and will happen at the End Times. It's not for today. That is exactly what Wonder Woman (and satan) want you to believe. There's no war. Nothing to look at here, people; move along.

The enemy of your soul has one agenda: to kill, steal, and destroy. These aren't my words; they're the words of Jesus:

> *"The thief's purpose is to steal and kill and destroy. My purpose is to give them a rich and satisfying life"*

(Jn. 10:10 [New Living Translation]).

Why would Jesus say this if it wasn't true?

The enemy, who originated Wonder Woman's lies and labels, is out for blood. Your blood. He wants to steal what you do have, kill your faith, and destroy your joy. The enemy of your soul is not happy when you step out of your comfort zone, out of complacency, and into the fray. You are going to have to fight if you want to be set free.

Faced with that truth you can either retreat and go back to Wonder Woman who holds you captive, holds you back, and holds you down. Or, you can arm yourself for battle.

God, through Paul in his letter to the Ephesians, put it this way:

*"For we are not fighting against flesh-and-blood enemies,*
*but against evil rulers and authorities of the unseen world,*
*against mighty powers in this dark world, and against evil spirits*
*in the heavenly places"*

(Eph. 6:12 [New Living Translation]).

You won't hear *that* verse turned into a peppy Sunday school chorus. That's some heavy, dark stuff. And it's real. Real enough to be scary.

But God has not left us without hope in this battle. He goes on in the same chapter to give us all we need to wage war and kill Wonder Woman.

*Therefore, put on every piece of God's armor so you will be able to resist the enemy in the time of evil. Then after the battle you will still be standing firm. Stand your ground, putting on the belt of truth and the body armor of God's righteousness. For shoes, put on the peace that comes from the Good News so that you will be fully prepared. In addition to all of these, hold up the shield of faith to stop the fiery arrows of the devil. Put on salvation as your helmet, and take the sword of the Spirit, which is the word of God.*

(Eph. 6:13-18 [New Living Translation])

If you've spent any time growing up in the church, you've heard these verses before. If you don't believe you are at war, those verses seem filled with cumbersome and unnecessary accessories. Like that pretty belt that only shows off how thick your waist is. Useless! But armor isn't useless if you are in a battle; it's essential for survival.

Now that you know you are in the battle, and you are setting out to kill Wonder Woman, this wardrobe will be vital to your victory and freedom. Without it, you may end up a casualty of war and feel like giving up when you've just begun to advance.

Let's take a closer look at our battle wardrobe so we know how best to use the equipment God gives us to fight in this war.

## BELT: TRUTH

Trust God's truth—not the world's, not Wonder Woman's, not your own. Truth is the belt that holds everything in place. But what is truth?

Truth is only found in God and in His word, the Bible. Many people today believe the lie that the Bible is some antiquated prose of made-up stories. That is exactly what the enemy of your soul wants you to think. Satan himself quoted scripture (Mt. 4:1–11). Even he knows its powerful truth.

Grab onto the truth of God found in His word. You don't have to understand it all—no one does—but you do have to have a source of truth that is solid and absolute.

Without God's truth (the belt) in battle, you might end up with your pants around your ankles (and nobody wants to see that!).

## BODY ARMOR: GOD'S RIGHTEOUSNESS

We need to arm ourselves with God's righteousness because our own righteousness is like a filthy rag (eww! Let's not go there). Righteousness, simply translated, is right living. Yet, our own good works (right living) aren't righteous enough. We need the righteousness of Christ as our body armor or else the enemy will pierce our vital organs with the lie that we aren't good enough.

It may be that we aren't good enough, but Jesus within us is. Jesus's righteousness is something we get to wear once we become His. We intentionally clothe ourselves in it (Rom. 13:14). We choose Jesus's righteousness over our own, because His is superior.

How much time do you spend picking out your clothes in the morning? We must be just as thoughtful and intentional in clothing ourselves daily in our body armor as well.

## SHOES OF PEACE: THE GOOD NEWS

Don the Good News—the GREAT News—of Jesus's atoning sacrifice. Because Jesus took our place on the cross and put our sins on Himself, we have peace with God, and the peace of God. Think about that: peace with God, and the peace of God everywhere you set foot.

Peace is a rare thing today. Peace in the world, our workplace, our homes. Imagine taking peace with you as you walk through your day.

Peace in the midst of a battle is a powerful thing. I have never fought in a literal war, though I have relatives who fought in World War II, the Vietnam War, and the war in Iraq. I don't know of any soldier who has peace in the midst of their fighting, but God offers us peace in our daily battles. Don't you want that?

## SHIELD: OF FAITH

Your belief in God's goodness and His love toward you will put out the fiery arrows that seek to pierce your heart with doubt. Faith is believing. Faith is putting all your weight on God's character and promises and moving through life knowing that they are true.

Wonder Woman shoots flaming arrows of doubt at you all day long. She wants you to doubt God, to not take Him at His word. To believe her lies instead. She wants you to doubt His unconditional love for you and attempt to live up to her labels instead.

The only way to douse those false, burning projectiles is to raise your shield of faith high in front of you. Let your faith quench the fires of fear and doubt on the battlefield.

## HELMET: SALVATION

This is your own salvation experience. Once you come to Christ for forgiveness and salvation, no one and nothing can take it away. You belong to God now and nothing you say, do, or think can change that. The enemy loves to get into our minds and speak lies like, "If you were really a Christian . . ." The helmet protects our minds from such nonsense.

There are some faith communities who teach that you can lose your salvation. Salvation you can lose isn't true salvation. Salvation is the result of God's plan and power, not our own (Eph. 2:8–9). It's a gift you can't give back. If you can't save yourself, you can't unsave yourself either.

Wonder Woman would like you to believe you have that kind of power: the power to lose your salvation. Like any post-salvation sin isn't covered by the blood of Jesus.

The surety of your salvation is the helmet that protects your mind. Our minds are crazy things. We can convince ourselves of anything if we aren't careful. Our minds need protecting. God gave us this helmet of sure salvation for a reason. He knew we'd need it.

Protect your mind from Wonder Woman's lies. Wear your helmet.

## SWORD OF THE SPIRIT: THE WORD OF GOD

The Word—God's Word—is your only offensive weapon against the opposition in battle. Jesus used the Word of God to battle the enemy in the wilderness (Mt. 4) and it worked! If you only read God's Word when you go to church on Sunday, you won't be able to wield the sword in battle.

Getting into God's Word daily is like taking fencing lessons from the Holy Spirit. You learn when to lunge and when to parry. You discover how to attack and how to disengage.

Don't underestimate the power of this piece of heavenly equipment. God's Words brought the universe and our world into existence. He said it and it came to be. If His Word is powerful enough to create billions of stars, beautiful flowers, fish, and fowl, then it is powerful enough to help you wage war daily in your own life.

Put on this whole armor every day. Soldiers in battle don't wear their protective gear when they feel like it; they put it on first thing in the morning and sometimes wear it all day and all night.

With this snazzy wardrobe, you are now equipped to kill Wonder Woman. Once dressed and ready to go, remember that you are not alone.

"This is my command—be strong and courageous! Do not be afraid or discouraged. For the LORD your God is with you wherever you go" (Josh. 1:9 [New Living Translation]).

God said these words to Joshua right before he entered the Promised Land where he would face numerous battles. God goes with you into the fray. He accompanies you with His power and might.

Now armed for battle, you are ready to kill.

 **Let's be honest:**

*What has kept you from believing you are in a battle?*
*Do you believe it now?*
*Are you armed for the battle ahead? If not,*
*what steps do you need to take to get armed?*

## Kill the Lies and Claim the Truth

Wonder Woman's superpower strength is in her lies and labels, and our blind belief in them. The next step in killing her is calling out those lies and replacing them with God's truth.

Go back to the first chapter where we defined Wonder Woman. In the questions following each type of Wonder Woman, I asked you to list the lies you believed from each. Go back and do this if you haven't already. You need to know which lies and labels you believe if you intend to kill Wonder Woman.

Here's a list of the most common lies I see women falling prey to (myself included). They encompass every area of our lives. By calling them out, we kill them. By replacing falsities with God's truth, we deal Wonder Woman a fatal blow.

# The Perfection Lie

Perfection is a myth, a lie, a label from every Wonder Woman in our lives.

The house is meticulously clean. The kids are always on their best behavior. The budget always balances with a little extra left over at the end of every month. The jeans from high school still fit. The meals consist of only healthy choices made from scratch. Work is so rewarding it can hardly be called work.

Does this sound like your life? No, me neither.

So let's ask the obvious question. If no one actually has a life that fits that description, why are we so obsessed with trying to create one just like it? We are wearing ourselves out trying to create a perfect life, and a perfect life is just impossible.

Why is the need to have everything "just so" a bad thing? What's wrong with striving for excellence?

God's Word says, "But you are to be perfect, even as your Father in heaven is perfect" (Matt. 5:48 [New Living Translation]).

It does, but according to the Greek Lexicon, this "perfect" refers to completeness, maturity, and the idea of being finished. This is an inward maturity brought about by God's finished work through His Son, Jesus Christ. This has nothing to do with a clean house and a size six dress.

> **We were never meant for perfection
> on this side of heaven.**

This lie of achieving a flawless life is destructive, futile, and results in frustration. It's destroying your life, consuming all your energy, and holding you captive.

How?

It leads to discontentment.

When we strive to be perfect on this side of heaven, we are telling God we can do it better on our own. We don't need His grace after all. We are saying our idea of a perfect life is better than His idea of what He has planned for us. We are telling God we are not content with what He has given us, but instead want to have more. The problem is: more is never enough.

God says in His Word, "Yet true godliness with contentment is itself great wealth. (1 Tim. 6:6 [New Living Translation]).

Discontentment is unbelief in God's ability and His desire to provide what you need.

The children of Israel wandered in the wilderness for forty years. During those years, the majority of them were what I call Negative Nellies. They grumbled and complained about what they didn't have. They claimed to prefer slavery in Egypt to freedom with God, all because they were discontent. They were captive to the perfection lie while God was trying to set them free.

Discontentment leads to frustration.

We become disillusioned and lose heart when we attempt to be and project a persona, and life, of perfection. Why? It's impossible to achieve. The goal posts keep moving. There will always be someone with a more "perfect" life than you. A Wonder Woman life. Just when you think you are getting to perfection, it gets redefined.

"You must have the same attitude that Christ Jesus had" (Phil. 2:5 [New Living Translation]).

What was the attitude of Jesus? He was humble, obedient, loving, and content. He was never frustrated with the call God placed on His life, even though it meant having no place to lay His head.

Discontentment takes your eyes off what matters.

Did God send His Son to die on our behalf so we could have a clean house? I think we both know the answer to that one.

It is the eternal that matters, not the temporal. We are just passing through this life on the way to our real home. When we focus on creating a perfect life here, we lose sight of the perfect life to come. Our heart becomes divided and lost. Our passion for God is replaced with a passion for stuff and self.

"Set your affection on things above, not on things on the earth" (Col. 3:2 [New Living Translation]).

That verse in Colossians isn't a suggestion; it's a command and it shows where our treasure lies. Let's rebel against this perfection myth. Let's see it for what it is: a Wonder Woman lie from the pit of hell intended to distract us from what matters most.

## ⭐ ⭐ Let's be honest: ⭐ ⭐

*Are you willing to have an imperfect house, imperfect children, and an imperfect body in exchange for a perfect Father/daughter relationship with your God?*
*Which ideals of a perfect life do you need to delete and replace with what God has for you instead?*
*Are you willing to let go of your affections on earth and set them on things above?*

The result of naming and letting go of the perfection lie will be a dagger in the heart of Wonder Woman. It will result in peace and freedom for you, and you will receive more than anything this world has to offer.

### God doesn't want your perfect life; He just wants your heart.

Do you see how we called out a Wonder Woman lie and replaced it with God's truth? That is how we start to kill her.

# The Self-Worth Lie

If you are anything like me, you spend more time and energy thinking about your mistakes and short-comings than you care to admit. You ask God why He made you a certain way or gave you certain attributes you think are subpar.

God gave me a big nose. I'm not kidding, it's huge! And even after growing into it a bit as an adult, it still looms disproportionately large on my otherwise small head. It was the object of much ridicule as I grew up and resulted in me having a complex about it at a young age. I couldn't understand why God didn't give me a cute button nose like all the other girls I knew.

We all have a Wonder Woman lie we have believed about our appearance, attributes, and abilities. I have met so many women who are always putting themselves down, filling in the blanks of:

"I can't _____."

"I'm not good at _____."

"I don't have the gift of _____."

"I'm not _____ enough to _____."

How insulting this talk must be to God's ears when He hears His daughters tell Him He made a mistake.

God says through David in Psalm 139, "How precious are your thoughts about me, O God. They cannot be numbered!" (Ps. 139:17 [New Living Translation]).

While we are busy bashing ourselves, God is thinking about how wonderful we are.

You are a rare treasure. God only made one of you with your unique gifts, talents, personality, and abilities. He was intentional when He created you. He didn't make a mistake. He doesn't make junk. When we are self-deprecating and let our insecurities get the best of us, we are believing a Wonder Woman lie. We are telling God He messed up.

When is the last time you had a positive thought about yourself? When did you last thank God for one of your attributes or characteristics? As women, we sometimes mask our insecurities in the shroud of false humility. We think it is wrong to speak well of ourselves. We don't want to come across as bragging, conceited, or self-absorbed.

There is a difference between praising yourself and praising God for yourself, His creation. David understood the importance of praising God for the creation of himself:

"Thank you for making me so wonderfully complex! Your workmanship is marvelous—how well I know it" (Ps. 139:14 [New Living Translation]).

David praised God for how He made him. Are you willing to do that instead of allowing Wonder Woman to determine your worth?

##  Let's be honest:

*Do you spend most of your "self-talk" time bashing yourself? Do you have a*
*hard time accepting a compliment because your self-worth*
*is not based on God's truth?*
*God only makes good things. What is one thing about yourself*
*for which you can praise God today?*

Call the Wonder Woman self-worth lie what it is, and replace it with the truth that God broke the mold when He made you. In His eyes, you are the best! You are amazing just the way you are, the way He made you to be.

Another lie dead, another truth in its place, another wound to Wonder Woman.

# The Guilt Lie

Guilt is a powerful thing.

- •It can bring you to your knees.

- •It can haunt your days.

- •It can hold you back.

- •It can drive you crazy.

The guilt lie isn't the kind of guilt you feel when you offend God. That kind of guilt is healthy. We should feel bad when we do something wrong. That kind of guilt should drive us to our knees in confession to God and restoration of our fellowship with Him.

The Wonder Woman guilt lie exists when you feel guilty for not doing enough. For going to work and leaving your kids at home. For losing focus at work because you are thinking of your kids. For saying "no" to a request because you're tired. For eating that second piece of chocolate cake instead of salad.

I don't think there is a woman out there in the world who hasn't experienced this lie of Wonder Woman's. And on those days you don't feel guilty, in comes the guilt for not feeling guilty!

What is guilt? Guilt is nothing more than self-condemnation. It comes from within and from without, but certainly doesn't come from above.

So how is a woman of faith supposed to handle this toxic destination to Guilt Island?

## WITHIN

Guilt comes from our own expectations of ourselves. We have some idea or picture of what kind of woman/mother/wife we should be. The Actual Wonder Woman steps in and holds us captive to our own demands. When we don't live up to our own ideal picture, we succumb to guilt. This type of guilt is a flesh wound from a flesh mind.

## WITHOUT

The Actual Wonder Woman continues her assault as society drills into us what a "woman" looks like. Family members let us know when we are doing things "wrong." The Spiritual Wonder Woman paints a picture of what a "godly wife/mom/woman" should look like. These are the lies and labels of Wonder Woman. When we don't measure up to all these messages from her, we pack our guilt bags and head on a trip to Guilt Island.

Why? Because pleasing others becomes more important than pleasing God.

Both paths are destructive. Both lead to guilt trips, and both leave us feeling defeated and inadequate. We are held captive—held back and held down—and then made to feel guilty about it on top of everything else!

So what are we to do?

Take a detour . . .

. . . to the foot of the cross.

Go to the cross; confess for both your sins and your self-condemnation. Confess your belief in lies and labels of inadequacy to the only One who knows you and your heart. The One who knows your struggle and desire for approval from others.

You will stand alone at the foot of the cross, the symbol of God's mercy and grace.

When the woman caught in adultery was brought before Jesus, she had a reason to feel guilty (Jn. 8:1–11). She was guilty, she had done wrong. But Jesus didn't condemn her; He forgave her. Her accusers left one by one, and the only person left facing her was Jesus. And His opinion of her was the only one that mattered.

The accusers from within and without will be nowhere in sight when you gaze on, and take in, the beauty of God's sacrifice on your behalf. When you view with your heart the reality that God does not condemn you, you will no longer condemn yourself.

"So now there is no condemnation for those who belong to Christ Jesus. And because you belong to him, the power of the life-giving Spirit has freed you from the power of sin that leads to death" (Rom. 8:1 [New Living Translation]).

The next time guilt comes knocking on your door and asks you to go for a ride, send it packing and go to the cross. Wonder Woman wants you to obsess about pleasing others. God wants you to obsess about Him. God is your only audience. The audience of One is waiting for you, and He is the only audience that matters.

## Let's be honest:

*How many times did you feel guilty today?*
*Did your guilt draw you closer to God, or further from Him?*

Self-condemnation guilt is the result of not forgiving ourselves for our mistakes. When was the last time you forgave yourself?

If we hold onto guilt instead of the cross, Wonder Woman wins. Recognize the guilt lie, replace it with the truth of God's perfect forgiveness. I think Wonder Woman is starting to feel the pain now.

# The Success Lie

Success is one of those hard-to-define things. It means different things to different people in different stages of life.

- To the stay-at-home Mom, success may be maintaining her sanity during the school break.

- To the working woman, success may be getting everything crossed off her list before crawling into bed.

•To the entrepreneur, success may be having enough cash to meet payroll for the month.

Wonder Woman has handed us even more definitions of success:
•A bigger, better home.

•A thriving company.

•A best-selling book.

As women of faith, we are not bound by Wonder Woman's definitions of success. We are not even bound by our own personal definitions of success.

There is only one definition of success that matters, and that is God's.

Has God defined success? You bet. Only you won't find it in some success guru's webinar or a book from *The New York Times* best seller list. You'll find it in a person. Success, God's way, is written in the life of His Son, Jesus.

You might be thinking: "Wait a second—Jesus had a ministry that only lasted about three years, and resulted in a shameful death with all His followers deserting Him when He needed them most. You call that success?!"

I don't.

But God does.

How can that be?

God's definition of success is different. Not only is it different, it's perfectly different. Here are three ways God defines success:

### 1. Success Isn't About Action

Before Jesus ever performed a miracle, God called Him His beloved Son with whom He was well-pleased (Mt. 3:17). Before He accomplished anything noteworthy, Jesus pleased God.

God's idea of success isn't about what Jesus did, but about

who Jesus was. Jesus was God's Son, we know that. But more importantly, Jesus knew who He was, and whose He was. Jesus knew who He belonged to. He didn't need to do anything to prove it.

What about you? Who do you belong to? Are you defined by what you do? Are you a boss, a worker, a mom, a wife? Is your identity wrapped up in Wonder Woman's labels about what you do instead of who you belong to?

God wants us to know we are already successful if we belong to Him.

No other action required. Success isn't about being the next Elizabeth Elliot, Billy Graham, or George Mueller. In God's mind, our biggest success is belonging to Him.

## 2. Success Isn't About Position

Even though Jesus was called the King of the Jews, He didn't live like a king. Jesus laid down the position He had with the Father as God, and took on the position of a servant instead. He changed from ruler to servant, doing only and always what the Father asked Him to do (Phil. 2:7).

In order for God's plan of salvation for mankind to succeed, Jesus had to surrender Himself under God's authority, instead of insisting on being the King He is. Jesus was fine with taking orders from God. He even allowed Himself to be insulted and tortured by the ones He created.

What about you? Do you demand your rights? Do you insist that you deserve to be treated according to your position? Are you willing instead to take the role of servant in every area of your life?

God thinks being a servant is being successful. In fact, when it comes time for God's Kingdom, those who were in the least position will be lifted up to a higher status than those who were top dog here on earth (Mt. 20:26–27).

### 3. Success Isn't About Self

In Wonder Woman's eyes, success is defined by what we acquire and build. It is about building an empire, a legacy, a bank account, a tribe of followers. All these things serve us. Success easily becomes all about us. According to God, success is defined by what we do for others.

Jesus didn't just lay down His life, He laid it down for the good of all, even the ones who choose not to believe in Him. There is no greater act of love and selflessness than to give up your life to save someone else's. That is how God defines success. Wonder Woman defines success by what we accumulate. God defines success by what we give away.

What about you? Do you hoard what God has given you? Do you hold back your time, talent, and treasure because they are too precious to you, when giving them away could benefit someone else?

Success, to God, is giving up yourself and your own desires so He can use your life to bless others. It's about letting it go and giving it away.

Can you see now how Jesus is the ultimate expression of success God's way?

The only definition of success we need concern ourselves with is the life and character of Jesus. Everything else pales in comparison.

 **Let's be honest:**

*What does success mean to you?*
*When will you know you have achieved it?*
*Is success for you based on position and possessions?*
*Is your definition of success based on Wonder Woman's lies, or God's truth?*

Let go of Wonder Woman's definition of success, and cling to God's instead. When you do, you will kill another lie, and Wonder Woman suffers another blow.

# The Comparison Lie

This powerful Wonder Woman lie comes from all three Wonder Women forms: Mythical, Spiritual, and Actual.

Do you ever notice how much we compare ourselves to each other? Forget the media and the advertising industry; we do it to ourselves. Fill in the blanks with whatever thought crossed your mind today:

"They are better at _____ than I am."

"She's smarter, prettier, wealthier, happier, _____."

In fixating on what others have to the point where such a comparison defines us, we disparage the gift God created when He made us.

We are all guilty of falling into the comparison lie. It's a lie that holds us in place, keeping us from God's highest and best intentions for us.

Theodore Roosevelt said, "Comparison is the thief of joy."

Let me say that again: "Comparison is the thief of joy."

Remember that the enemy of your soul is a thief, first. Think about it. How many times, after comparing yourself to someone else, did you walk away feeling uplifted and encouraged, ready to take on anything that lay before you?

Most likely you walked away feeling incapable and uninspired. By demeaning ourselves, we insult our Creator:

*How foolish can you be?*
*He is the Potter, and he is certainly greater than you, the clay!*
*Should the created thing say of the one who made it,*
*"He didn't make me?"*
*Does a jar ever say,*
*"The potter who made me is stupid?"*

(Isa. 29:16)

If God wanted us to all be the same, with the same gifts and abilities, He would have made us as such. We would all be walking through this earth, looking the same, acting the same, and accomplishing nothing in the process. What a boring place that would be!

God created you, me, each one of us, especially for His purposes, for His glory, and for His pleasure.

"Thou art worthy, O Lord, to receive glory and honor and power: for thou hast created all things, and for thy pleasure they are and were created" (Rev. 4:11 [King James Version]).

You were made for God's pleasure. You bring Him joy just as you are. He rejoices over you with singing. He created a good thing when He made you. He created you with a purpose and a plan.

Look at what He said to Jeremiah: "I knew you before I formed you in your mother's womb. Before you were born I set you apart and appointed you as my prophet to the nations" (Jer. 1:5 [New Living Translation]).

God knew what Jeremiah's job would be before he was even born. The same is true for you as a working woman of faith. God planned for you to be in the workplace. He planned your whole life. He has gifted and equipped you to do the job He has called you to do in the place that He has called you to. What a joy to take that in by faith and believe it! Not because I say it, but because it is true.

Wonder Woman wants you to compare your life to someone else's.

She wants you to spend your time and energy wishing you were someone else. She wants you to waste your life wishing for someone else's.

God's truth wants to show you the unique life He planned for the unique you.

## God won't give you grace for someone else's race.

Run your own life race. Call out the comparison lie for what it is: a farce. A cheap substitute for God's masterpiece.

When I was a little girl, my mother bought me a cross-stitch pillow pattern to make for my grandmother (I am not crafty at all, so the pattern was a good idea!). When I finished the hours of stitching with multiple colors of thread, the back of that pillow top was a mess! It was a jumble of thread that didn't make any sense to the human eye. But when I flipped it over, I saw a beautiful picture in the multicolored threads. My grandmother treasured that pillow and kept it on her couch for years.

Our life is like that cross-stitched pillow. On this side of heaven, we see a mess of threads and knots. But when we get the view from the other side, we will see the most beautiful life! One better than anything we could have created. Only in heaven will we understand completely the pieces of our lives that were all part of God's plan. It won't look like anyone else's life, and we'll be glad for that! When we see our lives with heaven-eyes, we can see them for the masterpiece they are.

God says, "For we are God's masterpiece. He has created us anew in Christ Jesus, so we can do the good things he planned for us long ago" (Eph. 2:10 [New Living Translation]).

God calls you a masterpiece. A work of art. The original Greek word for masterpiece is *poema*. A poem. You are God's poem. Isn't that a beautiful thought?

## ★ ★ Let's be honest: ★ ★

*How often do you compare yourself to others?*
*How do you feel afterwards?*
*How do you feel when you read about being God's masterpiece?*

Let this truth sink into your heart and release yourself from the comparison lie. Another hit to Wonder Woman and you are free to live your unique life with holy confidence!

## The Work Lie

This insidious little lie is straight from the Spiritual Wonder Woman. How many times have you left church hearing that the work you do outside the home is important to God? My guess is zero, or close to it.

According to my survey of working women of faith, 57 percent of the respondents said their church did not attempt to address the issues of women who work outside the home, and another 21 percent said it was only addressed sometimes. That leaves a mere 22 percent that felt there was at least an attempt by their faith community to address working women's issues.

In the faith community, Wonder Woman has infiltrated the ranks to tell us that our work only serves the purpose of providing money for God's "real kingdom work," like a new roof on the church, support to missionaries, and Sunday school supplies.

We leave church on Sunday and go to work on Monday feeling like what we do for the next forty or fifty hours of the week doesn't count for God. We leave our faith at home and church and never bring it with us into our work, or even view work the way God intended us to, as a gift from Him.

How do I know this? I took a survey of women from across the United States. When I asked women why they work, here's how they answered (multiple answers allowed):

- Financial security: 65%

- My work is my calling: 24%

- I enjoy working: 21%

- Desire for a career: 10%

- I don't know: 1%

- Other 4%

A whopping 65 percent said the reason they work is financial! That's a pretty sad reason to spend the majority of your time anywhere.

This Wonder Woman lie is destroying us and wearing us out. It leaves us fractured in our faith and wondering why we even bother. It's no wonder we are weary!

What if we are looking at it all wrong? What if we saw our work as something we get to do instead of something we have to do? What if we looked at it as a gift given to us? A gift from the hands of God? Because that's exactly what it is.

Work is a gift from God. This gift of work is both for us and for Him.

How is work a gift from God? Look at all the great benefits it supplies:

## SKILL-BUILDING:

God gives us gifts and abilities, and enables us to gain more gifts and abilities if we wisely use the ones we have. Without the gift of work, there is a lot we wouldn't be able to do in our world today. Work affords us an avenue to develop the natural talents, abilities, and gifts God has given us. In turn, the use of our God-given skills and abilities helps us to see the value God sees in us. Being able to do something, and do it well, makes us feel good about ourselves. Not in a prideful way, but in a way that makes God proud.

## PURPOSE:

Work gives us purpose, a reason to get up in the morning even when we would rather stay in bed. God knows it's not good for us to stay in bed all day. Work gives us a sense of accomplishment, the feeling that we added something to the world that day.

## PEOPLE:

Yes, people can often be a difficult aspect of work, but they are always something we need. If we stayed alone every day, we would become miserable, isolated, and lonely. God knows we need others, and that others need us, so He gives us the gift of work so we can have a daily community.

How is God's gift of work meant for Him? Doesn't God own it all and have it all? How could He benefit from me working?

God desires us to enjoy our work. He didn't give us this gift because He thought it would make us miserable. He gave us the gift of work because He loves us and knows what is best for us. He knew He could use the gift of work to carry out His purposes in us, and through us.

### God uses our work as an avenue for sharing Himself.

God could have angels flying through the sky to tell people about Himself, but He chose to use us instead. One way God can use us to tell others about Him is through our work.

Look at all the people you come in contact with over the course of a year. The multiplier effect of having us in a work environment, surrounded by other people, gives God more exposure than if we were to stay home alone, wearing our jammies (although there are days when I want to do just that!).

God uses our work to bring Himself glory.

Adam and Eve worked in the perfect garden setting. They were to tend the Garden of Eden and take care of the animals. God made us for work and He made work for us.

Who gets credit for Adam and Eve's beautiful garden? God does. Our work showcases God's glory and proclaims His greatness to the world—at least it can if we kill the Wonder Woman lie that our work doesn't matter to God.

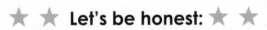

## ★ ★ Let's be honest: ★ ★

*How would your Monday to Friday change
if you looked at your work as a gift from God
instead of some forty-year punishment in cubicle oblivion?
Is this the first time you considered that your work matters to God?*

Kill the lie that your work doesn't count. It does. Not because you think it does, but because God says it does. This one is a big hit to Wonder Woman!

# The "My Plan Is Better" Lie

There's pressure from a young age in our society to decide what our lives will look like, even though our brains are still developing. Ask any five-year-old what they want to be when they grow up. Their answer is usually something fanciful and far-fetched. By the time that same child is fifteen, they are expected to have a practical plan in place for what they will do after high school graduation. Mythical Wonder Woman fills our young heads and hearts with fantasies. The Actual Wonder Woman tells us we are failures if we don't have our whole life mapped out by the time we get a diploma.

Within the faith community, we receive this same kind of pressure from Spiritual Wonder Woman. Missionaries and preachers speak at our churches, pull our heart and guilt strings, and suddenly we think that anything less than vocational ministry must be short-changing God and holding back His Kingdom here on earth. When I was in fifth grade I wanted to become a nun. I loved God and wanted to serve Him. In my young mind, I thought being a nun was the only way I could do that (then sixth grade came and I decided boys were too cute for me to be a nun!).

Once adulthood happens and we aren't all those "things" that we dreamed we'd be, or people said we should be, we feel like failures. We feel "less than" and wonder why we are the only ones who can't get it together.

This is the Wonder Woman lie that you must have a plan for your life, and that your plan is better than God's.

I recently sat down for dinner with a group of college students who were there to learn proper eating etiquette in workplace situations. Some of them knew what they wanted to do with their education; some did not. But it brought me back to my days as a young college student. When I was eighteen, I thought I knew what I wanted to do, but God had better plans.

I shared with the students a little of my God journey and let them know what they want for their life is nothing compared to what God has in mind.

You can make all the plans and preparations you want for the future. You can get degrees, training, and mentors. You can take classes, self-assessments, and poll friends and family members. But when it comes down to it, you don't control the future. God does. Nothing you do will result in your desired outcome unless God allows it. But the Wonder Woman lie says that if we follow God's plan for our lives, He'll make us do something we hate. Wonder Woman says we need to be in control of our own destinies.

Yet, God's truth says you and I don't call the shots. God does. As followers of God, we don't get to tell God what we are going to be when we grow up. He tells us. He doesn't tell us the whole plan all at once, and that's what makes us nervous. Lets be honest, though—we couldn't handle it if God showed us our entire life plan at once anyway. We'd run away screaming and hide out in the hills.

What God does is reveal His plan for our lives step-by-step. He says, "Go straight here," and we go straight. He says, "Turn left at the next corner," and we do it. Then He reveals the next step, and the next, and the next, until He calls us home. Life is not about some destination; it is about an unfolding of God's plan for your life.

Think about Mary, the mother of Jesus. She had plans to marry Joseph and live a nice quiet life in the suburbs of Nazareth. She had no idea what God had planned for her. She would have never imagined that she would get to be the mother of the Messiah, and then watch Him die. It wasn't all sunshine and roses, but if you ask Mary about it someday, she will say that her plan for her own life did not compare to the life God gave her.

I told more than one student at the dinner that if anyone would've told me twenty-five years ago what I would be doing now, I wouldn't have believed them. Nothing compares to God's plan for my life. And now I am filled with excitement for what He has planned for the next twenty-five years and beyond.

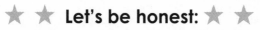

### ★ ★ Let's be honest: ★ ★

*How old were you when you had a plan for your life?*
*As you look at your life, can you see the fingerprints of God's plan? Or is it all smudged up with your own fingerprints?*
*Are you living your plan for your life or allowing God to give you His?*

His is better, you know. In fact, nothing compares to it!
POW! ZOOM! OOF! Another hit to Wonder Woman!

# The "You Are Unloved" Lie

I went to Haiti last fall. I held sick and dying babies. I saw people, made in God's image, living in deplorable poverty. One of the things God taught me when I was there is that everyone wants to feel safe and loved.

It's universal, our need for love. God put this need in us to draw us to Himself, since God is love (1 Jn. 4:8).

Unfortunately, we try to fill the love need with things we think will bring us love, but rarely can. We attempt to find love in unhealthy relationships with people, food, substances, shopping, and you name it. We stuff all this stuff in us, trying to fill that love need. Why?

Because we have believed the Wonder Woman lie that God couldn't possibly love us. He can love really godly, good people, but not us. We just don't feel loved by God sometimes. I went through this recently myself, even though I should've known better.

I was sitting there on a cold metal chair in the basement of our church. Sunday school was about to start. I didn't feel like being there. I wanted to be home in bed, with the pillow shielding my eyes from the light streaming into the bedroom window. It had been a few long weeks, and the culmination of many life trials had taken their toll on my heart.

I didn't feel loved by God.

I had spent the last few days talking a lot to God. Less talking and more asking. Maybe asking is too soft—I had been begging. Begging for answers and guidance. Begging for help. All I heard in response were crickets. The silence made me feel unloved.

So there I was, sitting in church, not wanting to be there and assuming God's silence meant He didn't care. "He's given up on me. He's disappointed in me," I thought.

Have you been there before? Have you had trial upon trial in quick succession and called out to God, only to hear silence? Did you feel alone? Unloved?

At that moment, in my low place, the song started. A song I have heard and sung a thousand times without even thinking about it. The words poured out of my mouth by rote, but my heart felt them for the first time in a long time. My voice poured forth and mingled with my tears as I sang:

**Jesus loves me, this I know. For the Bible tells me so.**
**Little ones to Him belong.**
**They are weak, but He is strong.**
**Yes, Jesus loves me.**
**Yes, Jesus loves me.**
**Yes, Jesus loves me.**
**The Bible tells me so.**

In that little chorus, so simple and pure, I sensed God's presence and I knew He loved me. Not because I felt it, but because He said so.

**God loves you, whether you feel loved or not.**

You don't have to feel loved. You don't have to deserve love. You don't have to do love. You are loved.

Because God says so.

God's Word is full of "says so's." They're called promises. God says:

- He loves you with an everlasting love (Jer. 31:3).

- You are dearly loved (Rom. 5:5).

- God has a great love for you (Rom. 5:5).

- Nothing can separate you from His love for you (Rom. 8:35, 38–39).

- His love controls us (2 Cor. 5:14).

- His love gives everything to you (Gal. 2:20).

- He loved you before He made the world (Eph. 1:4).
- His love gives you life (Eph. 2:4).
- His love for you is wide, high, long, and deep (Eph. 3:18).
- His love is too great for you to understand (Eph. 3:19).
- His love has chosen you (1 Thess. 1:4).
- His love comforts you (2 Thess. 2:16).
- His love for you is out of this world (1 Jn. 3:1).
- He showed His love to you (1 Jn. 4:9).
- He loved you first (1 Jn. 4:10).
- He is love (1 Jn. 4:16).
- His love keeps you safe (Jude 1:1).
- His love has freed you (Rev. 1:5).

Take a moment to look up those verses above. Write them on a Post-It Note and place them around your house so you can continually kill this Wonder Woman lie. So you can *know* you are loved, even when you don't feel it.

Feeling loved or unloved has nothing to do with the reality of God's love for you. Feeling loved or unloved cannot stand in the way of God's truth that you are loved.

This lie is crucial to kill. Love is what God's redemptive plan is based upon. His perfect love for us. It is the central need from which flows everything else in our lives.

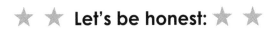

## ★ ★ Let's be honest: ★ ★

*What "stuff" do you use to try to fulfill your need for love?*
*Do those things fill your need for love?*
*How would your life change if you believed (not felt) God loved you?*

This one is a lethal hit to Wonder Woman.

# The "Don't Be Radical" Lie

This lie is one of the most powerful. It's a cheap-shot tactic of Wonder Woman called "good enough" faith. It's the lie that says: Don't be a holy-rolling, Bible-thumping woman—no one likes people like that. You go to church, volunteer, do good things, and that's enough. Don't get radical.

Jesus was radical. He was so radical His enemies had Him killed. The early apostles were radical—so radical they were called "little Christs," and were turning the whole world upside-down. The early church-goers were so radical that they were persecuted, killed, and scattered.

Wonder Woman has filled our hearts and minds with the belief that radical faith isn't necessary. Good enough faith is sufficient. This lie holds us captive to an ineffective faith. It holds us back from making a difference in the world with our faith. And it holds us down from obtaining faith that soars.

That's not God's truth and it isn't freedom. God's truth about faith is a radical, surrendered, non-conforming faith. A faith that changes our lives and the lives of those around us.

God calls us to be living sacrifices to Him that aren't copy-cats of this world. That sounds pretty radical to me. Let me show you radical faith that frees.

## RADICAL SURRENDER

*"And so, dear brothers and sisters, I plead with you to give your bodies to God because of all he has done for you. Let them be a living and holy sacrifice—the kind he will find acceptable. This is truly the way to worship him"*

(Rom. 12:1 [New Living Translation]).

## God doesn't want our some, He wants our all.

And He deserves our all.

This is a beautiful verse when you break it down, but our response is often less beautiful.

God, through the apostle Paul, begs, pleads, cajoles, urges, and implores us to present our bodies (which includes our hearts, minds, dreams, wills, etc.) to God as a living sacrifice.

After all, look at what God's mercy has accomplished in us (Rom. 1–11). This surrender, God says, is the only true and proper worship response to all He has done for us.

A living sacrifice is just that: a sacrifice that isn't dead. There are a few examples of living sacrifices that may help us understand how we are to be a living sacrifice that stays on the altar:

1. **Isaac**: In Genesis 22, Abraham is asked by God to go and sacrifice his son in a place that God will show him. Abraham rises the next day and takes his son and some servants to travel to the mountain for this event. Long story short, when Abraham has his knife lifted to slay his son, God stops him.

But what about Isaac? We don't get much information about Isaac himself, except that at one point in the journey, Isaac asks his father, "We have the wood and the fire, but where is the sacrifice?" Did Isaac get nervous due to his father's silence? Was he curious? We don't know. We do know that he was around thirteen years old—old enough to ask, and old enough to know something was fishy about this trip.

Scripture says Abraham bound his son and laid him on the altar; I don't think Isaac put up much of a fight. This wiry teenager could've out-run his over one-hundred-year-old dad. I can only surmise that Isaac let his father tie him up and prepare to sacrifice him to God (and we think we have issues from our childhood!).

Whatever happened, Isaac had to be somewhat willing to sacrifice his own body for what he believed God had in store for him. Isaac didn't try to jump off the altar and run away. At least, not that we are aware. But Isaac wasn't the only living sacrifice . . .

2. **Jesus**: This is the ultimate example of what a living sacrifice looks like. Jesus was willing to give Himself, His body, His spirit, to the Father to provide a bridge between God and all mankind. Jesus didn't have to do this. He chose to do this. Jesus was a willing sacrifice.

Jesus put Himself on the cross for you and me. The Jewish leaders may have sentenced Jesus to death, the Roman soldiers may have nailed Him to that cross, but it was Jesus's love for you and His obedience to the Father that kept Him there. If there had been any other way to provide a way back to God, Jesus would have taken it. But there wasn't, so He didn't.

Hebrews 12 says that Jesus was willing to suffer and die. A willing sacrifice. A living sacrifice. Jesus could have stopped the whole crucifixion at any moment, but He didn't. And aren't you glad!

What does it mean for you and me to be willing sacrifices? No one is taking us up a mountain, laying us bound upon an altar with a knife poised to end our lives.

No one is nailing us to a cross, bloody and suffering, to save all mankind.

Yet God is clearly asking us to present ourselves as willing, living sacrifices.

Sacrifice, by definition, is giving up something in exchange for nothing.

We often grasp tightly to what we think is ours, not realizing that it was never ours in the first place. It all belongs to God. He bought us with a price (the blood of His Son) and our lives no longer belong to us, but to Him.

God will not force you to give your body, your life, as a living sacrifice. It has to be your choice, and yours alone. It must be born from a desire to worship God in response to all He has done for us.

**Surrender is not a battle of the wills;
it is a radical act of worship.**

Often, we desire to give God our all, to completely surrender. It may be at the end of a church service or during a particularly trying time. We then decide later that the sacrifice is too great and jump off the altar (we are a living sacrifice after all, not a dead one).

What happens when you jump off the altar and decide you aren't willing? God waits. He shows you His grace and His love and calls you to sacrifice again. So you return, grateful for another opportunity to worship Him through surrender, and you climb back up on the altar, surrendering again.

Complete surrender is a process, not a one-time event. It is a daily act of worship.

Complete surrender starts, then stops, and then starts again. The key is to keep surrendering.

Don't stop. Just because you fail once doesn't mean that God's desire to have you as a living sacrifice is void. Come back to Him and surrender again. He will never turn you away. Each act of surrender is an act of worship.

That is one part of radical faith. The other part is what happens when we do surrender. It involves saying no to the Wonder Woman lies and labels and letting God transform you from the inside out.

## RADICAL TRANSFORMATION

*"Don't copy the behavior and customs of this world,
but let God transform you into a new person by changing the way you
think. Then you will learn to know God's will for you,
which is good and pleasing and perfect"*

(Rom. 12:2 [New Living Translation]).

Wonder woman says, "Follow me, and be like me." God says, "Let me transform you into something new!"

The verse above is a direct command from God. The words "don't copy" can be exchanged for "conformed." This is the idea of being pressed into a mold. God doesn't want us to allow the world (Actual Wonder Woman) to press us into its mold. God doesn't want us to believe Wonder Woman; He wants us to kill her so we can experience a new life with Him. A radical life, an abundant life, a victorious life.

Notice that God does the transforming, not us. When we choose to not let the world influence us and Wonder Woman lie to us—but instead allow God to transform us—then we learn to know God's will for us.

Wonder Woman tries to mold us from without; God desires to change us from within. Change from within is the only change that lasts. These changes influence others, creating a desire in them to have the same type of relationship we have with God.

So what about mimicking godly people? Is that wrong?

As believers, we do the same thing with those in the faith community. We mimic those whom we admire, those whose lives exemplify godliness. We often imitate and look up to religious leaders such as pastors, missionaries, and worship leaders. We tend to think, "If only I could be like them, then God could use my life." If we aren't careful, these can become Spiritual Wonder Women in our lives. It may not be bad to look up to a godly person and try to imitate their principles, but it can become a trap and a hindrance if it allows Spiritual Wonder Woman to press you into her mold.

God has made you unique. You are the only one of you that He ever made. There is not a version 2.0 of you. He did that for a reason. You were the only one of you that could fulfill what He has planned for you. But that's going to require a radical transformation.

As you allow God to transform you by renewing your mind—and killing Wonder Woman and her lies—the verse above shows the promised result. You will KNOW God's plan and will for your life.

If we are busy trying to be someone else—godly or not—we miss God's will for our own lives. We won't have the impact in our world that we are destined to have.

Allow God to transform you into the one *He* designed you to be. Mimic Jesus and forget the rest.

**There's no competition when you seek to imitate God.**

 **Let's be honest:**

*Does the idea of radical surrender scare you? Why or why not?*
*What are you willing to give to God as an act of worship?*
*Your plans*
*Your schedule*
*Your career path*
*Your family*
*Your ideas*
*Your money*
*Everything*

What is one area of yourself or your life you want God to radically transform?

The radical truth response to the "don't be radical" lie hits Wonder Woman hard. She suffers another blow, and you gain freedom.

# The "Your Heart Is Wicked" Lie

This one may take you by surprise. This Spiritual Wonder Woman lie is deeply entrenched in many faith communities, and has been in your heart without you knowing it.

This lie says that your heart is desperately wicked. There's even a verse to back it up:

"The human heart is the most deceitful of all things, and desperately wicked. Who really knows how bad it is?" (Jer. 17:9 [New Living Translation]).

Chances are, if you spend any time in a church setting, this isn't your first time hearing this. Maybe you've heard whole sermons based upon that one verse, taken out of context.

Remember when I said that lies often have an element of truth to them? That's how they can be so deceptive and destructive. It's true that the hearts of unredeemed people are wicked. They have no choice; they are slaves to sin and under the control of the enemy. Of course their hearts are wicked.

But for the redeemed heart, it just isn't so.

So what is a redeemed heart? A redeemed heart has:

•Repented of sin.

•Accepted God's free gift of salvation through grace.

•Belief that Jesus took their place and their punishment for sin when He was crucified.

•Belief that He rose from the dead with victory over sin, death, and the grave.

•Received Him into their heart for redemption.

That kind of heart has now become the dwelling place of Jesus. Jesus has redeemed, ransomed, and transformed that heart at the moment it made the choice to believe and apply the free gift of salvation from God. Jesus doesn't dwell in a wicked and deceitful place. He has cleaned your heart-house, and now your heart is good.

*"Your heart is good, and it matters to God."*
*—John Eldredge*

That is how John Eldredge puts it in his book *Waking the Dead.*⁵ Your heart is good and it matters to God. Read that again. Let the truth of it soak in.

Now say this out loud, "My heart is good and it matters to God." Say it again. Again.

I know what you're thinking: "If my heart is now good, why do I still fall short and sin?"

Your heart is good, but your flesh is not. You are still battling with your sin nature—the "old man," your lower self. God, through Paul, in the book of Romans expressed this:

"For I know that nothing good dwells in me, that is, in my flesh. For I have the desire to do what is right, but not the ability to carry it out" (Rom. 7:18 [English Standard Version]).

Notice that Paul didn't say that in his heart nothing good dwells. We battle *for* our heart; we do not battle *with* it. But we do battle with our flesh.

Jesus put it this way:

"Watch and pray so that you will not fall into temptation. The spirit is willing, but the flesh is weak" (Mk. 14:38 [New International Version]).

Our flesh is weak. Our redeemed heart is good.

Can you see now? Can you see how damaging this Spiritual Wonder Woman lie/label has been to your life? Do you see why you need to kill it and replace it with the real truth of God?

## ★ ★ Let's be honest: ★ ★

*Have you been told your heart is wicked?*
*Do you have a redeemed heart? If not, go re-read what it means to have one. Ask God to redeem your heart.*
*Are you doing battle with your heart or your flesh?*
*Say it once more, "My heart is good, and it matters to God."*

Another blow to Wonder Woman; she's taking her final breaths.

## Finish Wonder Woman Off

Is there a Wonder Woman lie from Chapter One that you don't see in the categories of lies listed above? It fits in there somewhere.

Have you believed the Wonder Woman lie that you need a man to complete you? That would fall under the "unloved lie."

Have you believed the Wonder Woman lie that you need plastic surgery or weight loss to be valuable and feel good about yourself? The truth is in the "self-worth lie."

Have you believed the Wonder Woman lie that the kind of Christianity I am talking about is a little too extreme? Re-read the "don't be radical lie."

Whatever Wonder Woman lie is on your list, there is a truth from God to replace it. Think you have a lie that doesn't fall into any of the categories listed above? I challenge you to call it out and search God's Word for His truth to replace it. God's Word has an answer and truth for every opposing lie from Wonder Woman. Seek the truth. God will show you where to find it. He's not hiding the answers from you. He wants you to kill Wonder Woman and be set free.

Once you've gone through your list of lies, called them out, and replaced them with God's truth, you can declare Wonder Woman dead.

Time of death? Now.

BAM! Wonder Woman is dead. Congratulations! You killed her! Cue the music and do a happy dance!

And now that she's dead, you can finally be free. Set free to walk in freedom, fight for freedom, and set others free.

# PART TWO

# SET
# FREE

I hope you went through the tough work of killing Wonder Woman by killing her lies and replacing those lies with God's truth. This is a required step to freedom.

Nature abhors a vacuum. If you kill the Wonder Woman lies but don't replace them with God's truth, you will find yourself back where you started. You'll be held captive by new lies, held back by a half-dead Wonder Woman, and held down from soaring in your faith.

**_Killing the lies and claiming the truth is_**
**_what sets you free._**

Jesus Himself said that, "Then you will know the truth, and the truth will set you free" (Rom. 8:32 [New International Version]).

According to Jesus, a person can't be spiritually free unless and until they know the truth found in God's Word. If you did that—killed the lies and claimed the truth—then Wonder Woman is dead. She no longer holds you as her prisoner. You have been set free.

Do you feel it? Are you starting to sense a lightness, a relief?

What does it mean to be set free?

## FREEDOM THROUGH CHRIST

Unfortunately, many people have an erroneous concept of freedom. They look at freedom as a license to do whatever pleases them. As women of faith, Jesus Christ has set us free. That is true freedom.

"So if the Son sets you free, you are truly free" (Rom. 8:36 [New Living Translation]). Jesus sets us free to live life to the fullest, without encumbrances, according to God's perfect plan for us. Now we are free to be who God made us to be, not who Wonder Woman says we are.

## FREEDOM THROUGH THE HOLY SPIRIT

The Holy Spirit guides us to understand God's truth and leads and empowers us to live it out. When we walk in the Spirit, we gain victory over our flesh and the lies of Wonder Woman. This spiritual understanding leads to freedom.

"For the Lord is the Spirit, and wherever the Spirit of the Lord is, there is freedom" (2 Cor. 3:17 [New Living Translation]).

Now what? Now that we are set free, what do we do with that freedom?

There are three steps we can take in our newfound freedom to help us remain free:

1. Walk in Freedom

2. Fight for Freedom

3. Give Others Freedom

We'll unpack these in this next section so you remain free from the nasty Wonder Women you just killed.

# CHAPTER FOUR

# WALKING IN FREEDOM

Walking denotes movement. It's the deliberate action of putting one foot in front of the other. Walking in freedom is no different. It starts with learning *Whose* you are, and living (walking) according to that truth. Self-discovery helps us learn who we are; discovering what it means to belong to Christ helps us learn *Whose* we are.

## Learn *Whose* You Are

You no longer belong to Wonder Woman, and her labels and lies. Instead, you belong to Christ in freedom, but you must learn what that means. Who are you now that you are free in Christ? We explored some of these truths when we killed Wonder Woman's lies, but that was just the beginning. There is a vast, unsearchable amount of truth about who you are in Christ. It will take the rest of your life to uncover it. This life-long learning is key to walking in freedom.

Take time to learn *Whose* you are. If you are only spoon-fed God's Word once every Sunday, how do you expect to walk in your newfound freedom?

Think of God's Word as an all-you-can-eat buffet of spiritual yumminess.

All-you-can-eat meals and buffets are popular. There are pizza buffets, all-you-can-eat fish fries, breakfast buffets, and "Chinese" buffets (complete with self-serve ice cream machines). If you have ever been to one of these, you know how you feel when you leave: like doing nothing.

There's another way to eat more and do less. It has nothing to do with physical food and is the number one way to walk in freedom: It's the Bible. God's Word. The Holy Scripture. It's feeding on the Word of Life.

God's Word was created by God, through the Holy Spirit, as He moved men to write. It was created for us. God knew we would need something to guide us—a channel to communicate His heart with us, a tool for our growth. He chose His Word to do all those things.

Scripture is not just a historical record of ancient days and lives long passed. It is a living, breathing love letter to each of us and God still uses it for His purposes today.

But Jesus told him, "No! The Scriptures say, 'People do not live by bread alone, but by every word that comes from the mouth of God" (Mt. 4:4 [New Living Translation]).

God intended for us to feast upon His Word. To use it for sustenance. To enjoy it like I enjoy a good cannoli, savoring every morsel. Reading and thinking about God's Word is food for your soul.

## EAT DAILY

Too many believers eat once a week at church and wonder why they don't feel close to God. Or don't know how to deal with daily issues in their life. Or why they can't seem to find God's will for their lives. Or aren't set free from the Wonder Woman labels and lies.

## God didn't mean for us to eat only once a week.

Think about it. Your body gets hungry every five hours or so. It needs constant fuel to operate as intended. The same is true for your soul. In order for your spirit and soul to operate efficiently, you need to feed it daily, not just once a week.

If you are relying on a pastor to feed you, you are missing the point. God wants full custody of your life, not just weekend visits.

Start simply. Get up fifteen minutes early every day and read God's Word. Pick a chapter, or start by reading one chapter of Proverbs every day. God has conveniently broken up this book into thirty-one chapters (I don't think that was a coincidence).

Proverbs contains wisdom that can help you navigate your workplace, your relationships, your money, your time—you name it, and it's in there.

Just start somewhere. Don't try to tackle Leviticus on your first day. That is some rich food to start with. Pick one of the gospels to read through to get reacquainted with who Jesus is and what He said.

Just start, and do it daily. Feed yourself instead of waiting for someone else to do it for you. You will grow spiritually like you never have before. I guarantee it!

Over time you will find yourself getting up a little earlier to spend more time with the Word. You'll start adding in extra time to study or read God's Word, or even listening to it during your commute. What started as fifteen minutes for me is now an hour (or more). It includes reading through the whole Bible every year, journaling, and using other study resources. Funny thing, I don't miss that hour of sleep anymore. I'm too hungry (spiritually) to sleep.

Just start with fifteen minutes and go from there.

God's Word is transformational; you will be transformed if you read it.

## EAT REAL FOOD

Devotional books and Christian nonfiction (like this book) are great tools! But they are no substitute for the real Word. Have a few devotional books to read besides the Bible, but don't rely on them alone for your daily food.

Twinkies have fewer nutritional benefits than a spinach salad. Devotional books don't have the same benefit as reading God's Word.

Once you crack into the Word of God and make reading it part of your daily life, you will find that nothing compares to the real thing.

## SHARE WHAT YOU EAT

When I have a great meal somewhere, I love to tell others about it. A perfect blini or an amazing shrimp gumbo is worth telling someone about. The same is true with the spiritual food I eat. I love talking to others about what God is showing me in His word and how it changes my thoughts and my life.

It's hard to share about God with others in your workplace when you don't even know what His word has to say. But when you feed yourself, you will have plenty to share. After all, evangelism is one beggar telling another beggar where to find the Bread. And that Bread is Jesus. He said it Himself: "I am the bread of life. Whoever comes to me will never be hungry again. Whoever believes in me will never be thirsty" (Jn. 6:35 [New Living Translation]).

At this point, maybe you are asking, "Where's the 'do less' part? Right now all I see is a lot of eating, which only gives me one more thing to do."

Here's the amazing thing about eating up God's Word daily. It changes you.

•Where you once strived to do more, you will begin to rest in God's power.

•Where you once struggled with your shortcomings, you will find peace in God's forgiveness.

•Where you once attempted to do it all yourself, you will surrender to God's strength.

God's Word will begin to transform you into a person who finds joy in the midst of sorrow, calm in the midst of a storm, and victory in the midst of a battle.

THAT is the power of God's Word. By taking the time to feed yourself, God will do in you and through you all those things you have been trying to do yourself. And you will thrill at watching Him do it.

  **Let's be honest:**

*Do you think of the Bible as an antiquated history book, or a love letter addressed to you?*
*When is the last time you read God's Word on your own?*
*Do you feel hungry spiritually? What are you going to do about it?*

## Live What You Know

Once you've started learning *Whose* you are, you become equipped to live what you know. Instead of following Wonder Woman lies and labels, you start to be guided by God's truth. And God's truth cannot be contained. It will move from head-knowledge to heart-knowledge as you believe the words you read. Head-knowledge is learning something in theory. Heart-knowledge is believing and practicing what you learn. Heart-knowledge always results in action. What you believe is expressed in your actions sooner or later. You will start to live what you know to be true, not the Wonder Woman lies that you used to believe and live out. Those are gone because you killed them and replaced them with truth.

This isn't about following a list of rules and regulations. This is walking in freedom. There's a big difference between the two. Someone once said, "Love God and do what you want." The truth behind that is powerful.

When we love God unconditionally, our wants will line up with what He wants for us. Our desires change and our actions follow. Now we want what God wants, which is to live out in action what He has put into our hearts with His love. Living what we know isn't accomplished in our own power, but in God's. We exchange our puny power for God's mighty power working within us.

"For God is working in you, giving you the desire and the power to do what pleases him" (Phil. 2:13 [New Living Translation]).

God helps us live what we know. Rest in the knowledge of that truth. He not only helps us live what we know, but on days when we don't feel like living what we know, He also gives us motivation.

God is working in us, both giving us the desire and the power to please Him.

- God's power makes the hard stuff easy.

- Desire without power is fruitless.

- Power without desire is pointless.

God gives both. Why? Because God wants to see us walk successfully in the freedom He gives us. He desires to see us experience the power that comes from a life lived close to Him. He longs for us to see Him working in us, so that we can realize how much He loves us. He wants us to succeed in living what we know.

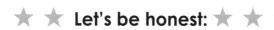

## Let's be honest:

*Do you have a lot of head-knowledge about God, but no heart-knowledge?*
*How do your actions line up with what you believe?*
*Do you ask for God's power to live what you know,*
*or are you trying to do it all yourself?*

# Love the Journey

When I go for a walk or run down our back-country roads, I don't do it out of drudgery or obligation; I do it because I want to do it. AND I enjoy every minute! I love to watch the wildlife and look at the landscape changing throughout the seasons. I take in the sights and smells and sounds as I go along. I enjoy the journey. That is the last part of walking in freedom: Loving the Journey.

God has some pretty cool things He wants to show you as you go through life. Little, private gifts meant only for you: a sunset that takes your breath away, a smile from a good friend, a song that lifts your heart, a smell that brings a happy memory. Small ways of showing His presence and love to you. Signs that He is on the journey of life with you.

### Enjoy the journey more than the destination.

•Enjoy watching God set you free.

•Enjoy learning new things about *Whose* you are.

•Enjoy the little victories of living what you know.

Walking in freedom with God is not a life sentence in asceticism and boredom. Walking in freedom with God is like walking around the circus or fair on your Dad's shoulders. He takes you through life in safe, loving arms, showing you amazing things along the way. Once in a while, you'll crawl off His shoulders and go your own way. Don't worry; He's waiting for you to return because He still has many amazing things to show you. Enjoy the journey with God, instead of trying to perform for Him or rush the process. This is walking in freedom, not running in freedom.

## 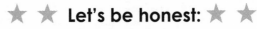 Let's be honest:

*Are you enjoying life's journey?*
*Do you notice God's private little gifts He is trying to give to you?*
*How much are you trying to perform for God instead of enjoying Him?*
*Do you ever run ahead of God?*
*Slow down and enjoy what He has for you today.*

# CHAPTER FIVE

# FIGHTING FOR FREEDOM

Remember when I told you that Wonder Woman (aka satan) wouldn't go down without a fight? Once you have gained your freedom from Wonder Woman and her lies and labels, you will have to fight to keep that freedom for the rest of your life.

Sounds like bad news, I know. I promise this is not a bait and switch tactic I just pulled on you. You killed her and her lies and replaced them with truth. You may have killed her in your life, but her deviousness remains in this world and keep others in bondage. Their bondage and her lies will rub up against you as you walk in freedom. Like those tagalongs or thistles that attach to your clothing as you walk through a field, Wonder Woman's lies and labels are sticky. You'll need to fight to keep them from binding to you.

Here's how you fight for your newfound freedom:

•Keep Killing

•Keep Your Heart and Mind

•Keep Advancing in Freedom

Your freedom is worth fighting for!

# Keep Killing

The armor of God we put on to go to battle with Wonder Woman is something you'll need every day going forward as you keep fighting for your freedom. Consider it the daily uniform you put on before you head out the door. What do you insist on wearing before you leave your house? Lipstick? Your glasses? A bra? I will not leave the house without a bra; it's just a thing with me! Whatever your essential "thing" is, it can't come close to being as necessary as your daily armor.

Those lies we killed—they will rear their ugly head again. The media will continue to pump out those Actual Wonder Woman lies. You will see a movie or read a book that has a mythical Wonder Woman label in it. You will hear another sermon on Proverbs 31 that will be a Spiritual Wonder Woman lie in disguise. It will happen.

The good news is that you'll now be able to spot the Wonder Woman lies and labels coming from a mile away. You have waged an up-close and personal war against those lies. You know the taste of freedom in Christ now. There is no way you are going back to letting Wonder Woman hold you captive, hold you back, and hold you down.

Good for you! You're ready for battle on a moment's notice. You're prepared, capable, empowered, and able to kill again.

When Nehemiah set out to rebuild the walls of Jerusalem with the few inhabitants left, the enemies of Israel set out to hinder them. They taunted and threatened the Israelite construction crew. They mocked their progress. But God's people under the leadership of Nehemiah would not be deterred from their important work. What did they do? They kept building the wall. Only from then on, they built it with a shovel in one hand and a sword in the other. They were prepared to defend and fight for their progress (Neh. 4).

The same is true for you. Yes, you killed Wonder Woman. Yes, you are now set free in Christ to be the woman He made you to be. And yes, you will protect your progress.

Only now, you are a more experienced fighter. You are a killer who has killed before, and you know what you need to do.

When another Wonder Woman lie comes your way (maybe one that you haven't yet dealt with), you can kill it quickly by calling it out and replacing it with God's truth. You won't let those nasty lies gain access to your heart and mind. You will nip them in the bud before they have a chance to bloom.

If you tend a garden, you know you have to remove the weeds when they are young or they will choke out the other plants. The same is true with killing new, or recurring, Wonder Woman lies that are trying to plant themselves in your life. Get them early, before they have a chance to take root and grow.

Keep killing, keep fighting, never give in, and never give up.

### ★ ★ Let's be honest: ★ ★

*Did you put your armor on today?*
*Have you noticed any new Wonder Woman*
*lies or labels trying to attack you?*
*What is one thing you can do daily to prepare for a possible battle?*

## Keep Your Heart and Mind

Two of the most essential organs in your body are your heart and your brain. You cannot live without them. Doctors can put you on life support if there is a problem with one or the other, but you aren't fully alive if either of them becomes injured beyond repair.

Your skull protects your brain from harm (a really thick skull in my case). Your sternum and ribs protect your heart. God placed protection over them because he knew how essential they are to your life. Yet, you do have a choice to protect your head and heart beyond your natural armor. You can wear a helmet when riding a bike or playing sports to protect your brain. You can exercise and eat a healthy diet to protect your heart from disease.

The same is true when it comes to keeping your heart and mind. You can make choices to protect them and help them stay safe and strong.

The mind is an incredible thing; just Google "amazing facts about the mind" if you don't believe me. A thought is a physical pathway in the brain. The more you have that thought, the deeper the groove of that physical pathway becomes.

If you continuously dwell on Wonder Woman lies, they become entrenched in your mind. To have a new thought, you have to stop thinking the old thought (Wonder Woman lies) and replace it with a new one (God's truth) to re-route the groove of that physical pathway.

God's Word backs up this physical fact with a practical tip: think on good things.

"And now, dear brothers and sisters, one final thing. Fix your thoughts on what is true, and honorable, and right, and pure, and lovely, and admirable. Think about things that are excellent and worthy of praise" (Phil. 4:8 [New Living Translation]).

Fix, or focus, your thoughts on true, honorable, right, pure, and lovely things and you will create new pathways. You can fight for freedom in keeping your mind by changing your thoughts when lies come along and focus on truth and good instead.

Another way to keep your mind is to prevent harmful lies from entering it in the first place. If you have a weakness for mythical Wonder Woman, then don't watch movies or read books that feed you those lies. If you are susceptible to Actual Wonder Woman lies and labels, you may need to cut out some people or media streams from your life to keep your mind protected. Be proactive and intentional about what your mind is exposed to. Put a mind gate up to keep out those things that have a negative influence on your thought life. Sometimes you make every effort to protect your mind and the lies find a back door entrance or sneak in through an open window.

When a Wonder Woman lie does comes into your mind, be swift to go to battle. The other day I was having a meet-and-greet phone call with an amazing woman that a friend recommended I connect with. As she talked about her work and mission, I noticed the Wonder Woman comparison lie start to creep into my thoughts.

Before I knew what had happened, my joy was stolen and I felt deflated. Instead of being encouraged by what God was doing in her life, I could only feel despondent about my own future prospects. Then ZING! I unsheathed my sword, called out that lie, and replaced it with the truth that God has a plan for my life that doesn't belong to anyone else. I've been fighting and killing Wonder Woman for twenty-five years and I still have to be on guard!

*"The unattended garden will soon be overrun with weeds; the heart that fails to cultivate truth and root out error will shortly be a theological wilderness."*
*—A.W. Tozer*

The heart is another matter. When we talk about the heart, we aren't talking about the physical organ, but rather the seat of our souls, the base of our emotions, the source of our lives.

*Keeping your heart is essential and necessary as you fight for your freedom.*

Our hearts are often:
- Vulnerable
- Tender
- Soft

They can also be:
- •Bruised
- •Broken
- •Hardened


As women, we are known for our hearts. Our hearts are said to be caring, compassionate, and sometimes cruel. What God says about our hearts is especially important for us, as women, to heed.

"Above all else, guard your heart, for everything you do flows from it" (Prov. 4:23 [New Living Translation]).

There are three parts to this loving direction:

**1. "Above all else"**

God places emphasis on this command. Above everything else in your life—your family, husband, kids, friends, workplace calling, and even yourself. Above everything and anything, guarding your heart is most important.


**2. "Guard your heart"**

This is the "what" that you are to do above all else—guard your heart. We are notorious for giving our hearts away. For letting other people and other things into them that will only cause us harm in the long run.

There are things in our hearts that have no business being there, all because we have not guarded them. We let in people who hurt us. We feed our hearts fantasies (Mythical Wonder Woman) that destroy us. We give our hearts away to people who don't deserve them. We allow them to wander from our God who loves us.

**God is the only one who should have full,
unrestricted access to our hearts.**

Guarding the heart is the action step of this verse. It means that we have to be proactive. We must stand sentry in front of our hearts with diligence and consistency. We must determine who and what gains access based upon God's Word alone.

There needs to be a secret password for anyone or anything to gain entrance to our hearts. We have to draw on strength from God to deny access to anyone or anything that God does not want in there. How do we know who and what God wants us to let into His territory of the heart? Ask Him. Read His Word, pray, and follow His lead.

There is a war going on for your heart, remember? A battle wages in the unseen spiritual realms with the goal of tearing you away from your God and His purposes for your life. Be ferocious in guarding what ultimately belongs to God. Don't let the enemy even get his foot in the door.

### 3. ". . . for everything you do flows from it."

This is the "why" behind the "what." Why should we guard the heart at all costs and above all else? Because from our hearts flows everything in life. If we set our affections on the wrong things, the wrong people, or the wrong thinking (Wonder Woman lies), we WILL end up going in the wrong direction and end up at the wrong destination.

Everything in our lives stems from the heart, so it stands to reason we have to be careful of who and what we let in as it is bound to come out, sooner or later. Garbage in, garbage out.

*If you are in a place in your life that you don't want to be, it's your heart that got you there.*

But God's grace is huge. You can have a do-over, a fresh start. Ask Him to cleanse your heart, forgive, and make it new. Then set about to guard what He has given you.

The first step is to set your mind and heart on the things of God. Second, commit to guarding what God gives you. Third, make it a priority above all else. This is how you protect your heart and mind as you fight for your freedom.

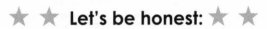

## Let's be honest:

*What deep groove (or physical pathway)
in your mind needs to be re-routed?
Which Wonder Woman is getting access to your mind?
Are you good at guarding your heart from people and things that harm it?*

Commit to keeping (and guarding) your heart and mind above all else.

# Keep Advancing

As you repeatedly kill Wonder Woman—and maintain your heart and mind—you *will* keep advancing. You won't be able to stop and nothing will be able to stop you.

But I'll let you in on a little secret. As you walk in freedom and fight for freedom, you will mess up. You are going to have days when you fail to kill the lies, forget *Whose* you are, and fail to live what you know.

You're human, not perfect. It's okay. You are not alone. We all mess up; we all make mistakes. I have messed up this freedom walk more times than I care to admit.

I'm not trying to discourage you or scare you; I'm trying to give you an honest look at reality so you are not blindsided when it happens. So you can keep advancing when it does.

Let's look at a few people in scripture that blew it big time. Some recovered and some didn't. Then we'll look at how to be one who recovers, gets back up after failure, and keeps going to the finish line.

## FAILURES WHO RECOVERED:

### Moses chose to hurry God's plan

Moses knew God had a plan to make him a leader of the people of Israel. Moses thought God was moving too slowly on that plan, so he took matters into his own hands. Sound familiar?

Moses killed the Egyptian who was oppressing his countrymen (Ex. 2:11–15), which forced him to go on the run. He spent the next forty years as a shepherd—a far cry from the leader of Israel God destined him to be. Moses got impatient and blew it.

### Jonah chose to run away from God

Jonah chose to disobey God's plan for his life because he didn't have compassion for people. Jonah knew God was merciful and he didn't think those people deserved God's mercy, so he ran away. Far away (Jon. 4:2).

Jonah tried to run from God and ended up with new digs—a fish belly—and left for dead. Jonah didn't like the way God worked and, as a result, he blew it.

### David chose his passion over God's purity

God brought David from shepherd boy to Israel's king. He had it all. In having it all, David got comfortable. In getting comfortable, David got careless. David let down his guard and fell victim to his own flesh weaknesses when he made Bathsheba, a married woman, lay in his bed (2 Sam. 11:2–4). It only got worse from there. In choosing comfort, David blew it.

## Peter chose fear over love

Peter was so afraid of what others thought of him and his association with Jesus, he denied even knowing Jesus. Peter feared what others would think of him. Peter feared the ridicule instead of leaning on the unconditional, unfailing love of Christ. Peter was afraid and blew it.

The good news about these four individuals is that they recovered after they blew it.

- Moses became the leader of the Israelites and led them to freedom.

- Jonah preached to the people of Nineveh and his warning saved an entire city from death.

- David ruled the nation of Israel and his second child from that union with Bathsheba was Solomon, the wisest man who ever lived.

- Peter became the head of the early church and preached the first message of salvation after the ascension of Christ.

- Each one recovered, but not without a cost.

- Moses spent forty years as a lowly shepherd.

- Jonah had to spend three days and nights in the belly of a fish.

- David had to bury his first child with Bathsheba.

- Peter had to look into the eyes of his Savior as he betrayed Him.

In spite of the cost, they did recover from their failures, mistakes, and blunders. They moved on to fulfill God's calling in their lives. Even today they serve to teach us by example and remind us that we are not alone when we blow it.

Before we look at how to recover when you fail, let's look at those who failed and never recovered at all—those who are only remembered for their failures instead of their victories over them.

# FAILURES WHO DIDN'T RECOVER:

## Saul let success go to his head

Saul was the first King of Israel. Big guy, big responsibilities. He'd come a long way from his start as a humble young man hiding from the spotlight (1 Sam. 10:21–23). Saul soon let his success and power go to his head. His pride was his downfall. Saul started with the power of God and ended up having God's Spirit taken from him.

## Judas didn't seek forgiveness

Everyone knows the name of Judas. The name is synonymous with betrayal. Judas betrayed Jesus, but he also spent three and a half years with Jesus. Judas betrayed Jesus, but he also knew that Jesus had the power to forgive him. Judas felt remorse and even admitted that he sinned, but he never went to the only One who could forgive that sin. Judas never sought the forgiveness that Jesus gave to so many and chose to stand by and watch his betrayal unfold. Judas took his own life because he couldn't live with his mistake (Mt. 27:3–5).

## Ananias and Sapphira valued wealth over honesty

This lesser known duo decided to lie to God to pocket a profit (Acts 5:1–11). Having some extra money was more important than telling the truth. All they had to do was tell the truth about the amount of money they received. Instead, they attempted to cover up their profits, plan, and purposes and ended up dead.

So how do you recover from your failures? How do you keep advancing when you blow it? How can you end up a part of the first group instead of the second? Here are a few tips on how to recover after you blow it:

### 1. Know your weaknesses

When you blow it (and you will), look for what set you off. What factors in your own human frailty contributed to you blowing it?

Shore up your foundation. Use your failures to learn more about yourself. Sometimes I mess up in ways that surprise me initially, but when I analyze the situation, I discover issues I swept under the rug instead of facing head on. Now I can take those issues, unpack them, and hand them over to God so they don't become tripping points for me in the future.

## 2. Ask for and accept forgiveness

Jonah was right: God is merciful and compassionate. God is slow to get angry and is full of unfailing love. It's an amazing thing to know that God is always ready to forgive. It's another thing to ask for that forgiveness. So many times we feel too unworthy of God's forgiveness to accept it. And the truth is that we are unworthy. We don't deserve God's forgiveness or favor, and we never will. But God gives it to us anyway. God offers it to us free of charge. All we have to do is ask.

"If we confess our sins, he is faithful and just and will forgive us our sins and purify us from all unrighteousness" (1 Jn. 1:9 [New International Version]).

The other part of forgiveness is forgiving yourself. When you ask for and accept God's whole forgiveness, believing it to be complete, it will be possible to forgive yourself as well.

> ### To forgive yourself,
> ### you have to first accept God's forgiveness.

So you messed up. Big deal. You've done it before and you'll do it again. But without accepting God's forgiveness and forgiving yourself, you won't be able to recover.

## 3. Get up and keep going

This one won't happen unless you do the second point—asking for and accepting forgiveness. Without forgiveness, both from God and yourself, you will stay bogged down in a pit of self-pity, right where Wonder Woman wants you to be. Self-pity leads to feelings of worthlessness and justification for blowing it some more.

You will fall down again, but if you get up one more time than you fall down, you can recover. Get up and keep going. Keep advancing in the truth God has told you in His Word. Keep in the Word. Keep praying. Keep spending time with God. Keep spending time with other believers who can strengthen you and hold you accountable in your weak areas.

Get up and keep going even if you don't feel like it. Our faith journey with God is not about feelings. It's about truth.

Don't let your emotions guide your recovery.

Emotions are fickle and deceptive, but God's truth never falters; it never changes or fails.

God wants you to recover when you blow it. God wants you to overcome the sin in your heart that led you to blow it in the first place. God wants you to be successful in your walk with Him. God is for you, not against you.

Do you remember the do-over? As a kid, if you didn't do well on your turn during a game, you could just yell authoritatively, "DO-OVER!" Immediately, you received a second chance to try again as if the mistake never happened. That's what God's forgiveness is like. God gives us a do-over every day.

> *Because of the Lord's great love we are not consumed,*
> *for his compassions never fail.*
> *They are new every morning;*
> *great is your faithfulness.*

Lam. 3:22–23 [New International Version]

I like to call this "the do-over" verse.

God loves to give us "do-overs"! Every time we mess up and come to Him and repent, He wipes away all stains of our shortcomings. God alone can declare a do-over on our behalf.

•With every new sunrise . . .

•With every admission of guilt . . .

•With every acknowledgment of inability . . .

•With every acceptance of humility . . .

. . . we face another chance. Another opportunity to rest in the grace of God, instead of striving in the rule of law. Another opportunity to admit that He is God, and we are not. He controls the universe and orders our steps. We get another opportunity to hide in the shadow of His wings.

The good news is: God's got you.

When I feel like I'm falling short, making no progress, or about to go off the deep-end, God reminds me that He's got this and He's got me.

On days that you struggle to kill lies and fight for your freedom, don't quit! Just get up, dust yourself off, and keep advancing.

 **Let's be honest:**

*Have you ever blown it big time?*

*How long did it take for you to go to God for forgiveness?*

*Which one of the Bible failures mentioned can you relate to the most?*

*What is a weak area of your life where you find yourself repeatedly failing?*

*Is there a past mistake you need to forgive yourself for today?*

# CHAPTER SIX

# LEADING OTHERS TO FREEDOM

One of the most beautiful things about being set free is you won't be able to keep it to yourself. You're free and you want everyone to know it! You see others held captive, held back, and held down by the Wonder Woman labels and lies. You want to lead them to freedom.

If it takes a village to raise a child, it takes an army to set women free. And you are now a part of that army. Lead others to the freedom you have gained.

## Be a Storyteller

The first part of leading other women to freedom is to tell your story. That's what I'm doing here. I'm not making all this stuff up as I go along. I have lived this; I have killed Wonder Woman and been set free to win at work and soar in faith. And I'm telling you how I did it so you can be set free and set other women free.

Take what you have experienced in your battle against Wonder Woman, in killing lies and claiming truth, and share it with the other women in your life. Tell your daughters, granddaughters, aunts, grandmothers, mother, friends, and anyone who will listen about what you've been through and how they, too, can be set free. Tell your story. Shout it from the rooftops! Call out the lies and proclaim the truth.

I recently did this with my own daughter. As a recent college graduate, she was believing the Wonder Woman lie that she wasn't good enough to apply for a certain job. I called out the lie. She went for it and got a job—not the one she applied for, but a better one suited to her gifts. It was amazing to see her go to battle with Wonder Woman and win. That is leading others to freedom.

We women need to help each other be successful in this thing called life. It's time we stop being competitive and catty about the shallow things of life. We are all on the same team and we all want to win. Why not help a sister out instead of putting her down? We need to help each other to freedom. Telling our story, warts and all, will help us get there together.

## Be an Example

People are watching you, and that attention will only increase once you kill Wonder Woman and are set free from her lies and labels. You will be different, and others will notice the difference. You will be the poster child for what killing Wonder Woman looks like.

Be a real example to those watching. Let them see your victories and your mistakes. If you don't share the bad along with the good, you risk becoming a Spiritual Wonder Woman to those who are watching. And you don't want to do that.

One role model of mine is a woman in my church who had polio as a teenager and hasn't walked since. She is an example of a woman who has been set free, even though she is confined to a wheelchair. She is an example of grace and encouragement—of one who trusts God, and maintains a sweet spirit in the face of trials and struggles. She is one of my greatest cheerleaders. She memorizes verses every week and says them to me. I know she prays for me, and I can move in greater freedom because of her prayers. Her own freedom inspires freedom within me.

Be a genuine, authentic example—*that* is how to lead others to freedom.

# Be Available

Every car needs a trailer hitch. Not because you have to haul around copious amounts of cargo on a regular basis, but because you never know when the need might arise. I put a hitch on my latest car because I thought I would be moving my college-aged kids back and forth. I've only used it twice and one of those times was for straw bales, not dormitory furniture. But it was there when I needed it. It was ready to pull whatever load I needed transported at the time.

The same should be said of us, as women of faith. We're there when we're needed. We are available and approachable to lead others to freedom.

Are you ready to be a trailer hitch to someone?

Think about it. A hitch:

•Pulls something along that can't make it on its own

•Carries a load

•Transports something to a better destination

•Leads the way, protecting the load

How about you? Are you a trailer hitch to someone?

**We all lead someone. In our workplace, home, church, or community. Everyone is a leader.**

Leading is influence. How we lead will determine the impact of our influence. Leading is not about having others follow you wherever you go and do whatever you do. Leading is about bringing others along into their full potential and freedom in Christ.

There are good leaders and bad leaders in this world and in our lives. Maybe you have a bad leader for a boss. Maybe you had a bad leader in your family growing up. Maybe you followed what you thought was a good leader in your church, only to find out later that they weren't so good after all. We can all pick out the bad leaders in our lives. But we can't always see the good ones. Look for one who is like that trailer hitch, then watch and learn.

- A good leader pulls someone along who can't yet make it on their own.

- A good leader carries a load.

- A good leader transports others to a better destination.

- A good leader leads the way, protecting the people who follow.

Jesus was a good leader. In fact, He was the perfect leader. He was a trailer hitch leader to anyone who followed Him. He led a group of disciples for three and a half years. He led thousands of people to turn to God. And has led billions more through the years. It was God's plan for His life: to lead others to freedom.

God's plan is for you to lead others to freedom too. To be a good leader for other women in your life. God's plan is for you to lead those in your life to Him, just as Jesus did. You won't be as perfect of a leader as Jesus was, but if you follow His example, you can't go wrong. You can be a trailer hitch to someone and make yourself available to lead others to freedom.

They need your story, your example, and your availability. Lead on!

## Let's be honest:

*What story has God given you to tell? How could that story set others free?*
*Find one opportunity this week to share your story*
*with another woman in your life.*
*Who has been an example in your life, leading you to freedom?*
*Are you available? Are you a trailer hitch to someone else?*

# PART THREE

# WIN
# AT WORK

What does work have to do with killing Wonder Woman? Or faith, for that matter?

First, more women are working outside the home than ever before. Recent labor participation rates of U.S. women range from 67.7 percent – 74.1 percent,[6] depending on the age group and which findings you view. Within the faith community, that number is 54 percent (I think that number is low; it's possible they included the Amish and Mennonites in their poll).

According to a study by the Institute for Faith, Work and Economics,[7] working women are pulling out of the church in big numbers.

This is due, in large part, to messages centered on men in business and women in the home. Here's what the study had to say about how the church is neglecting the needs of working women:

**"There's no way for us to see the constant spiritual warfare she faces in the workplace, her mission field. They are game-changers, bravely facing the corporate world and all the challenges that it holds."**

All women are working women. From sun up till sun down, we work. Whether that work takes place in the home, outside of the home, volunteering at your kids' school, or even in your place of worship. I do not favor one type of work over another. Yet, once a woman enters the workplace outside of the home, she enters new territory.

It doesn't matter what type of work you engage in outside of the home. From Burger King to the board room; part-time to full-time; just starting your first job, re-entering the workforce, or working through your retirement years; you need help to win at work God's way. We all do.

Additionally, women feel like their gifts and talents are often overlooked in the church. They may run a large corporation or supervise a team of employees, but they are rarely considered to head up a church committee and are often relegated to serving in the children's ministry.

Even though fewer women are attending church on a regular basis, their faith remains central to their lives. A study by the Shriver Report[8] entitled "The Challenge of Faith" found that many women want to connect their family, work, and faith. The report said faith helps provide daily encouragement and helps "in navigating life's complexities, as well as a way to unify [women's] different roles."

I can relate. Can you?

I speak to women everywhere who are clamoring for a message that connects all their life callings, instead of separating them. The church isn't providing it, for the most part. I am passionate about this connection. I started a non-profit three years ago to equip women of faith in their workplace calling. We are going to spend the next section diving into this topic of women, faith, and work as it is central to being set free, winning @ your work, and soaring in your faith.

If you recall from our list of lies to kill Wonder Woman, we talked about the work lie. This lie tells us that our work doesn't matter to God and His Kingdom here on earth.

The benefit of killing Wonder Woman is that you're set free to be the person God made you to be in every area of your life, including your work.

Wonder Woman wants you to separate your work from your faith. God's truth says He created you for work and work for you.

## Wonder Woman wants you to lose at work.
## God wants you to win at work.

In this chapter, we'll look at three ways to do this:

1. **Your Work, Your Ministry:** This section separates fact from fiction when it comes to your work as a ministry, which we are all called to be by God. It is a gift from Him placed within you, for your good and His glory.

2. **Your Work, Your Mission Field:** This segment deals with the subject of sharing your faith with those in your workplace so they, too, can be set free.

3. **Your Work, Your Minefield:** Here, we'll take those daily frustrations and look at scriptural hacks for how to deal with them God's way.

When you are through with this section, I pray you will see your work in a whole new light, free from Wonder Woman lies and filled with God's truth. You'll be ready to win at work in a whole new way.

CHAPTER SEVEN

# YOUR WORK, YOUR MINISTRY

What are you working for?

Do you work because you have to work?

Do you work because you want to work?

Do you work because God has called you to work?

Those are important questions to ask yourself. How you answer determines your level of fulfillment on a daily basis. It also gauges the long-term impact your work will have on you, and you will have in your workplace.

You don't have to work in ministry or even within a Christian organization for your work to be a calling. You only need to be obedient—to be where God has led you for your work—to have eternal ramifications that go beyond your bank account.

## The Faith/Work Disconnect

There is a disconnect in the faith community between work and faith. We're told from pulpits and in Bible studies that what we do from day to day at work doesn't matter much to God. The only thing that matters is what we do for God. Why can't your work be for God?

God Himself says, "Work with enthusiasm, as though you were working for the Lord rather than for people" (Eph. 6:7 [New Living Translation]).

He wasn't speaking only to those in vocational ministry; He was speaking to anyone who works. Our work can, and should, be done for the Lord's approval, not for people. Yes, our jobs provide us the ability to pay our bills, put roofs over our heads, and food in the fridge. But money is only a side benefit to doing whatever God has called us to do.

When the reason for working is financial, money becomes the focus. We obsess about it, work harder and longer for more of it, and get upset when someone else makes more of it than we do.

When we alter our focus from being about making money (or "having to work") to doing our work for God, it shifts our perspective. It adds meaning and purpose to our daily tasks, no matter the job title or company. We release ourselves from the trap of money and plunge into gratefulness. We see with a different set of eyes; we see God's heart behind the work.

You are not working for nothing!

When you view your work as God-appointed, regardless of what you do, work takes on new significance. Your work becomes God-ordained, God-anointed, and God-empowered, instead of some means to pay bills, which is separate from your faith.

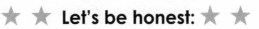

## ★  ★  Let's be honest: ★  ★

*Now that you are starting to have a new perspective about your work:*
*What are you working for?*
*Do you work for the Lord, or for people?*
*Have you been working for money, and leaving God out of the picture?*

# Work as a Gift

Work is a gift. You may not see it that way now, but hopefully you'll begin to change your mind and attitude about your work after reading this. We touched on this subject in the list of Wonder Woman lies, but let's dig a little deeper.

1. **Work is created by God, and it is good**

   Work is good because it is created by God. In the beginning, when God made everything we see in our world, He called it good. He also created a couple of people to take care of His creation: Adam and Eve. Their job was to take care of the garden. Sounds easy, right? Not when you have to tend to every plant known to man and name every animal! *That* was a job. The kind that takes dedication.

   God called everything He created "good." That includes the work that was waiting for Adam and Eve when He created them.

   Work was initially created by God, for us. The thing is, before the fall, work wasn't work. It was part of God's perfect plan for a perfect world. There were jobs to do, but it wasn't thought of as "work" like we think of work.

   After the fall, work became a thorn in Adam's side (Gen. 3:17–19). It was then work became hard work—work for survival that felt like, well, work. This was not God's original, perfect, and good intent. He created work, and called it good because He knew how important it was to Him, and to us.

   Just as God is in the business of redeeming our hearts, He is in the business of redeeming our work. God wants our work to be a blessing again, instead of a curse.

## 2. God created us for work

Not only did God create work for us, He also created us for work. We are hard-wired to do things, to accomplish tasks, to make things happen. It's in our DNA. It's how God created us.

Think about the last time you were bored. It probably hasn't happened since you were a kid. That's because we didn't have enough work to do as kids. Now, we are full of work and you'd probably be bored without it.

Work gets things done and, in the process, fills our God-placed need to accomplish something.

Work is a tool used by God, to bring about His purposes. Not only do we work to provide for our basic needs, but we find purpose and identity in our work. Ask anyone who's been unemployed for any length of time. They will tell you that loss of identity is the biggest struggle of being out of work.

We need work, and God knew we needed it. That's why He made it for us.

I believe that we will have jobs in heaven (or the new heaven and new earth), because that's how God made us. Besides, who wants to sit on a cloud and play a harp for all eternity? Boring!

*Work is God's gift to us;*
*what we do with it is our gift to God.*

## 3. Work is a gift exchange between God and us

Think of work as God's gift to us. Then think of our work as our gift to God.

Can you see how that change of thinking might affect your attitude to get up and go to work tomorrow?

God gave you this beautiful gift of work—He wired you for it and He knows it is good. Additionally, it can become a tool in His hand. A tool to provide your needs (because I haven't seen manna from heaven yet) and a tool to grow His kingdom.

As God provides for our needs through our work, He also provides us with the financial capacity to give to His work here on earth. God can use our work to financially meet the growth needs of His Kingdom on earth. It's not that God needs our money, it's that He wants children who are giving.

Not only is our work a financial tool, but a personal one. You know that co-worker you have who is going through a struggle right now and searching for God? You are there for that purpose, for that person.

Our work goes beyond paycheck and beyond purpose, right to people.

**God is not in the paycheck business, but He is in the purpose and people business.**

God is using you, in your work, to fulfill His purpose and reach people. THAT is why you are there. THAT is why you get up every morning and go to work. THAT is why you are called to your specific position in your specific place of employment.

It's all for God. That's His gift to us: our work has meaning beyond the task or title.

Our gift to Him? Show up. Give it your best. Your all. And then watch Him do amazing things with it.

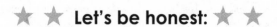

## ★ ★ Let's be honest: ★ ★

*What would happen if you altered your thinking about these three things?*
*How would your desire to get up and go to work change if you*
*believed these three things are true every day of your life?*
*How might you start to win at work with this new mindset?*

# Work Is Sacred

Did you know there is no separation between the secular and the sacred? To God, everything involving His children is sacred.

When we divide our lives into the two compartments—secular and sacred—we work against God. When we separate our work, or any part of our life, from our faith, we have fallen under the deception of perception.

I'll admit it. I am getting to that age where reading glasses are necessary. I get frustrated when I can't read the label of a package in the grocery store; I struggle to read price tags, and I can't pick up a book anymore without also picking up my glasses.

There is one place where I like my declining vision: the morning mirror. I like the way I look in the morning, until I put my glasses on! Then I see all the pores and imperfections in my skin, the road map of lines and wrinkles, the shining streaks of silver on the crown of my head.

It's all about perception. It's about seeing things with clear vision. It's about choice. I can choose to never wear my glasses and continue glibly living in my own reality of clear skin, no wrinkles, and lots of brown, gray-free locks. Sure, I would never have to see the wrinkles and gray hair, but I would also miss out on beautiful things as well. My view of life would be skewed and I would be deceived by my perception, missing out on the reality that is right in front of me.

The same is true for us, as women of faith. How we choose to see our faith journey with God will determine the benefits we receive from that relationship. If we see our relationship with God as a "church" thing, if we are "Sunday only" Christians, we are missing out on what God intended when He called us to Himself.

Many Christians today leave God at church and never bring Him home with them, never bring Him to work with them. They perceive the God relationship as something that is separate from the rest of their lives.

God doesn't belong:

- At work

- At school

- At the store

Consider what God said through Paul in Romans 12:

> *And so, dear brothers and sisters, I plead with you to give your*
> *bodies to God because of all he has done for you. Let them be a living*
> *and holy sacrifice—the kind he will find acceptable.*
> *This is truly the way to worship him.*

(Rom 12:1 [New Living Translation])

This includes our work. Our work becomes holy, sacred worship. It becomes a ministry. Romans 12:1 calls everyone into full-time ministry. That ministry may not be vocational, meaning you aren't a missionary or don't work at a church. But your work is ministry in God's eyes.

**When we separate our lives,**
**we live with a divided heart.**

With a divided heart, we live a divided life, and God's plan for our lives cannot be its fullest and best. God had so much more in mind for us when He redeemed us than outward, occasional religiosity. He wants access to every area of our lives.

Now that you can see the importance of an inclusive faith/work/life integration, how can you switch your vision to view your work as a calling, a ministry?

"Ministry" is from the Greek word *diakoneo*, meaning "to serve," or *douleuo*, meaning "to serve as a slave." Everything belongs to God. Your life is no longer your own; it belongs to Him. Thus, your life is sacred.

True to form and the free will God gives us, we can choose to surrender to His rightful ownership, or go our own way. Jesus had something to say about that:

"If you try to hang on to your life, you will lose it. But if you give up your life for my sake, you will save it" (Mt. 16:25 [New Living Translation]).

God is great about giving us choices. We can choose to hang onto our current life, or loosen our grasp and take what God offers instead. I guarantee that what God has in store is better!

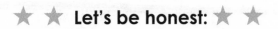

## ★ ★ Let's be honest: ★ ★

*What would happen if you*
*took the word "secular" out of your vocabulary?*
*How would your life change if you surrendered all to God*
*and considered everything sacred?*
*Would you rather see your work as a ministry or a drudgery?*
*A sentence, or a calling?*

If you want to win at work, you'll need to view your work as a calling from God Himself, straight to your heart.

# Work as a Calling

A calling can be defined as a strong inner impulse toward a certain course of action, or a strong desire to pursue a particular line of work.

According to a recent Barna research poll,[9] "only 40 percent of practicing Christians say they have a clear sense of God's calling on their lives." In further research, only 20 percent have a real sense of what God wants them to do with their lives.

These types of statistics break my heart. A calling is for each believer. A calling is God's way of guiding us to where He wants us to be. That can take place anywhere, with any skill set, at any time in your life. It's important to realize that you can have more than one calling in your life at the same time.

When we look at God's calling in our lives as some future goal to attain, an end point where we will finally be fulfilled or a position to work toward, we put limits and parameters on God.

God has a plan and a calling for your life. It may not always look like you think it should, but it will lead you to far better adventures than any you could have dreamed up on your own.

God longs to give us the desires of our heart:

"Delight yourself also in the Lord, and He shall give you the desires of your heart" (Ps. 37:4 [King James Version]).

It's true. Those desires of the heart are the desires that God put there, not the ones we come up with on our own. And that's a good thing.

Think of the desires you have for life as a string of plastic pearls. They may be shiny and nice and good-looking from far away, but upon closer inspection, it's easy to see that each "pearl" is not the real thing. They are fake. Shiny and worth nothing. God's calling for your life is like a real pearl—beautiful, unique, and rare. It's the kind of thing that only God can create. Your calling. Unlike anyone else's.

"For we are God's masterpiece. He has created us anew in Christ Jesus, so we can do the good things he planned for us long ago" (Eph. 2:10 [New Living Translation]).

You are His masterpiece. Think about that. Say that out loud to yourself: "I am God's masterpiece!"

## God lovingly and uniquely created you with a plan in mind.

I'm not talking about a career change. I'm talking about an attitude shift.

God planned for you to be where you are now, doing what you do now, before the foundation of the world. I'll admit: some days I don't feel like a masterpiece when I'm answering emails and phone calls, and working on spreadsheets. It doesn't matter what I feel like, it matters what His truth says.

• It is God that gives your work meaning.

• It is God that makes your job into a workplace calling.

• It is your faith in Him that makes that truth a daily reality.

The challenge lies before you to see your job in a different light. Why not start now?

Before you work your next shift, even as you are entering the building, say this simple prayer:

"God, you have called me to this place to fulfill your plan for my life and your purposes for the universe. You have brought me here by your providence and uniquely equipped me to do this work today. You gave me this job as a calling on my life and I want to honor you for that by doing the best work I can with your help today, and for your glory. Amen."

Then watch what God does with your workday.

Your heart will be aligned with God's purpose for your life and your attitude shift will allow you to view your job through God's eyes. It will no longer be a job, but a workplace calling. Ultimately, our work is not done to serve ourselves, but rather to serve God; our work can actually bring glory to God.

##   Let's be honest:

*What are God's current callings in your life?*
*(Remember you probably have more than one at a time.)*
*How can an attitude shift change the meaning of your work?*
*In your workplace calling, who are you serving? Yourself? Others? God?*

## Work with Purpose

When the perspective of our work shifts from work to workplace calling, it gives us a new desire to work with excellence. Now you'll want to go the extra mile and do more than you're asked to do. You'll want to do your best. Not for your company, your supervisor, or yourself, but for God.

> *Work willingly at whatever you do,*
> *as though you were working for the Lord rather than for*
> *people. Remember that the Lord will give you an inheritance as your*
> *reward, and that the Master you are serving is Christ.*

(Col 3:23–24 [New Living Translation]).

**Transformation begins when work becomes worship.**

Worship brings purpose.

"So whether you eat or drink, or whatever you do, do it all for the glory of God" (1 Cor. 10:31 [New Living Translation]).

Whatever you do, when it's done for God's glory, it brings purpose. It makes no difference if you're waiting on customers, teaching students, or writing reports.

Our work, surrendered to God, is worship to Him. It's something that lifts Him up and points others to Him. People of faith should be the best employees—the most productive ones in the whole company—because our work is worship.

Now, what was once "just a job" becomes a joy-filled reason to get up in the morning. What used to be a career becomes a call to serve the God of the universe as your true boss.

It all comes down to our perception, remember? The reality that everything we do can bring honor and glory to God. Do we view our work as part of that "everything?" And when "everything," including our work, is done for God's glory and honor, our work purpose becomes worship that is eternal.

## ★ ★ Let's be honest: ★ ★

*Do you consider your work to be a form of worship?*
*If not, how can you change that?*
*Have you ever prayed before you enter work,*
*surrendering your work to God?*

Make even the most mundane task an act of worship this week.

# Work with Passion

According to the *Merriam-Webster Dictionary*, passion is defined as "a strong feeling of enthusiasm or excitement for something or about doing something."

Is that the way you feel about your work?

One of my clients was a manufacturer of skid loader attachments. I am not passionate about equipment. I don't even own a skid loader. I don't get tingles over pallet forks, spreadsheets, and warranty issues.

I am, however, passionate about God. He has done everything

for me and I am constantly amazed by Him. I am compelled to give all that I am and all that I have back to Him as an act of worship.

That included making and selling equipment for a time. He called me to that work, in that place, for that season of my life. He equipped me to do it, so that He would be honored and glorified.

The purpose of going to work every day is to worship God through my work. It is my purpose (worshiping my awesome God through my work) that ignites my passion.

**"There are many things in life that will catch your eye, but only a few will catch your heart. Pursue these."**
—Michael Nolan

I get excited and enthusiastic about my work because God captured my heart.

I got excited to go make and sell equipment not because of what I saw with my eyes, but because of what I saw with my heart. I got excited because I saw God, not the work. I got excited because I wanted to worship this God who captured my heart.

God is worth it! His love is immeasurable and unconditional. Perfect and pure. That love drives me to do what He calls me to do, in whatever season of my life. And where God calls, I go. Because He loves me, and I love Him.

I'm ALL IN.

ALL? As in ALL?

Can't I just give a little and keep some for myself? How about half? Half for God, half for me. Sounds fair, right? How about 75 percent? That's pretty generous, I think.

Nope. ALL. Everything. That's the definition of full surrender and commitment. In fact, God commands it: "And thou shalt love the Lord thy God with all thy heart, and with all thy soul, and with all thy mind, and with all thy strength: this is the first commandment" (Mk 12:30 [King James Version]).

When we love God with all we are and have, God gives us so much more in return. He gives us:

•Peace

•Purpose

•Passion

•Pleasure

Why hold back? Give God your all. Be all in, for Him and His glory, and watch your passion level for your work rise. After all, you have the best boss ever.

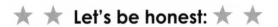

## Let's be honest:

*Are you passionate about your work?*
*Do you look forward to Monday, instead of Friday? Would you like to?*
*Are you ALL IN for the workplace calling God has placed you into?*

# Work for the Best Boss

Can you imagine walking into work and seeing God sitting in your boss's chair?

How would that alter your attitude toward your work? How would it change your excitement to get up and go into the office? How would it affect the quality of work you produce? Ultimately, God is your boss. Maybe He brought you to your current workplace calling to help your employer succeed. Maybe He brought you there to reach one of your co-workers or customers with His love and grace. Maybe He brought you there to teach you to depend on Him. Whatever the reason(s), you can rest assured that God brought you to your place of work for a purpose.

Part of being a working woman of faith is realizing that the work you do is not solely for your earthly boss or the company employing you. You work for the God of the universe, who put you into the position you are in. You work for God Almighty.

This reality that your work can be for the purpose of bringing glory to God will either be scary or liberating for you, depending on your relationship with God. If you know that God always has the highest and best intentions in mind—that He delights in you and rejoices over you—then working at your workplace calling to please Him will lighten your load of people-pleasing and self-induced stress. This truth can make every Monday better!

Consider this verse found in Zephaniah 3:17:

> *For the Lord your God is living among you.*
> *He is a mighty savior.*
> *He will take delight in you with gladness.*
> *With his love, he will calm all your fears.*
> *He will rejoice over you with joyful songs.*

Zeph. 3:17 (New Living Translation)

Wow. Just re-read that truth and let it sink in.

That is how your *real* Boss thinks of you every day. Whether you have a good day or a bad day. Whether you perform to your full potential or completely blow it.

God is good. He can't be anything except good.

•His goodness draws us to repent.

•His goodness gives us strength each day.

•His goodness has placed us into our job calling.

•His goodness forgives our mistakes.

His goodness lasts forever. Don't you want to please a boss who is good all the time? The effort to please God becomes easy when we think of His goodness.

You have the world's best boss! Literally.

When you realize it is God you are working for, then His approval is the only one that matters. Recognition, awards, promotions, success—all these are wonderful things. But are they too important? Does success, as defined by Wonder Woman's lies and labels, drive us? Are we more interested in human approval than we should be? As women of faith, we live for an audience of One.

## As working women of faith, we work for an audience of One.

People-pleasing is a fear-based Wonder Woman lie. We fear what others think of us and go out of our way to gain their approval. When the approval of our fellow human beings takes precedence over God's approval, we fall into a trap that is hard to get out of: the people-pleasing trap.

"Fearing people is a dangerous trap, but trusting the Lord means safety" (Prov. 29:25 [New Living Translation]).

Once we engage in performance approval as a measure of our self-worth, we become trapped in the cycle that never ends: pleasing others. We become tormented by what others think of us and tempted to do anything to gain their approval. It is this trap of people-pleasing that God declares is a danger for us.

Traps are a Wonder Woman scheme. Traps hold you where you are. Traps can hurt or kill. But if fearing people is a trap, what is the alternative?

Trusting the Lord means safety. We are safe from the trap of people-pleasing when we trust the Lord.

Trusting the Lord means putting all your weight on Him, to weigh each response from others through the lens of His great love for you. That way, no matter what others think of you (good or bad), your worth will lie in the only One whose opinion counts.

Your life is judged only by God, not others. Your approval rating is based on God's grace, not people's parameters. Your only performance review that matters is conducted by God Himself.

 **Let's be honest:**

*If you know God is your boss, will the way you do your work change?*
*Are you in a people-pleasing trap?*
*Where does the true worth of your work lie? In God? Your paycheck? Your position? Your accomplishments?*

## Work with Eternal Results

Everyone wants their work to count for something. To know that those thirty, forty, fifty hours they spend every week have an impact on more than just the bottom line (theirs or the company's).

Some choose a field where they feel they can make a difference, like teaching or healthcare. Others choose to work for companies that are making a difference through their products or services. But what if you work for a company whose main goal is to make money? What if you work in a field that offers no real impact in the world?

Can you still make a difference? Can you still influence the world? Or do you just go through the motions day in and day out, continuing to feel that your work has no meaning?

There are things in this world that satisfy, even if only for a moment:

- A steaming bowl of gooey mac and cheese

- A silky bubble bath

- A crackling fire on a cold winter's night

Yet even these delightful things are fleeting and forgotten. The same is true for our work. Even if you work in a "meaningful" industry, your weeks probably fly by quickly and you wonder if you have the impact you once did in your field. Or, you might run into someone you worked with years earlier and they struggle to remember your name or your position in the company.

Fleeting . . . and forgotten.

What if your work could have meaning regardless of your position or industry? What if your time devoted to your job—those thirty, forty, fifty hours each week—could have eternal impact? It can, and it should.

All it requires is a little bit of math. Apply the Impact Equation to any job to turn it into meaningful work:

# Purpose + Passion + Vision = Impact

**The Purpose** in our work (and everything else in life) is to bring glory to God through surrendering to God's will for our lives.

**The Passion** comes from worshipping God through our work. How exciting to think we can worship our Creator, God, through our daily work!

This type of purpose and passion allows us to look beyond spreadsheets and lesson plans to see more of the why (God's eternal plan) behind the what (our workplace calling).

**The Vision** is our ability to look beyond the here and now to the there and then. Looking with eternal eyes instead of earthly ones.

God has eternal plans for our work, but He needs us to open our eyes and see with His heart. What does God see when He looks at the work He has called us to do? Does He see the impact of a product or service? Does He see the company's bottom line?

God sees His creation. He sees you and all the people He has placed around you for thirty, forty, fifty hours a week. He sees the impact you can have on the lives of those around you. He sees hearts and souls—eternal ones. Not fleeting. Not forgotten.

Ken Blanchard,[10] a well-known business author and speaker, talks about labeling the "forever" and the "temporary." If you were to take Post-It Notes and go around your workplace labeling the things that are temporary and those that are eternal, you would find that the only things labeled "eternal" are other human beings. The spreadsheet, the lesson plan, the product or service—all temporary. Only people are eternal.

**Think of the impact you'd have for all eternity if you put on "God glasses" and could see the eternal.**

You hear many in the business world say, "It all comes down to people." It's a true statement. And as working women of faith, God has placed people around us who need Him. They need:

•His grace

•His mercy

•His forgiveness

•His love

They need a relationship with Him and you can show them the way.

## ★ ★ Let's be honest: ★ ★

*Are you ready to have meaningful work with eternal results?*
*Are you ready to use the Impact Equation?*
*Purpose + Passion + Vision = Impact*

May God grab hold of your heart and show you this truth. May you have a renewed sense of purpose, passion, and vision in your workplace calling. May God use you to have an eternal impact on the lives of those around you.

# Work with Wisdom

This may all feel a little weighty for you. Maybe viewing your work in this light gives you a feeling of greater responsibility. It should. Work is serious stuff to God. In light of all the wonderful and serious truth about doing our work God's way, you might be wondering *how* to work.

Wisely.

When Solomon was about to take over as the King of all of Israel, God approached him and said (basically), "Your wish is my command!" (2 Chr. 1:7–12). Solomon asked for wisdom to do his job. God granted Solomon his request and much more because he valued wisdom over money or fame.

God helps us to work wisely, to be worthy of the workplace calling He has given us.

Wise work means making the best use of the time and resources that God has entrusted to us. It means being wise in our decisions and interactions. Here are some other ways to work wisely, which will fulfill us and bring glory to God:

## 1. Work Hard

Working wisely means working, plain and simple. Some people do the minimum effort required of them to get by. That is not working wisely. If God were your boss (which He is), would the effort you put into your work please Him? Think about Jesus's parable of the talents and pounds (Mt. 25 and Lk. 19). There was a reward for the workers who put forth their best effort with the tasks that the master had entrusted to them. The only one who was reprimanded was the one who buried his talents instead of daring to let them grow.

On that day when you meet your Lord face to face, what would you rather hear?

"Well done, thou good and faithful servant!"

Or,

"You wicked and lazy servant!"

The work God gives us is like that. It's not about money or positions gained; it's about faithful stewardship. No laziness, no excuses, no blaming others. Just do your work to the best of the abilities and opportunities God has given you. *THAT* is working wisely.

## 2. Slow and Steady

### God doesn't expect you to work miracles. That's His job.

God wants you to do what He gives you to do in one given day. Trying to cram too much into a twenty-four-hour period will just lead to burnout, instead of the peace that comes from living (and working) for God alone.

Sometimes, the days drag on and you don't seeing the impact of your work. God is not working according to *your* timetable. Moses was forty years old before God called him to the job of leading all of Israel out of Egypt. Noah was 120 years old before he stepped onto the ark.

Don't rush God because He is never, ever, *ever* in a hurry. God has all the time in the world. In fact, He has all the time in eternity. You just keep trucking along, giving your best, day in and day out, and leave the results up to God. Slow and steady is how you work wisely.

## 3. Say "No" and Rest

The hardest two-letter word for women to say is "NO." We desire to do things, we long to help, and we are eager volunteers.

God made us that way so that we would be pliable vessels in His holy, loving hands. But God never meant for us to say "yes" to every request brought our way. By saying no to things that God has NOT planned for you, you are free to be faithful and steady in what God has called you to do.

You do not need to volunteer for every cause, attend every church function, or help every friend in need. Stop. Ask God if this request is part of His plan for your life and then follow His lead.

### Say "no" to the good to say "yes" to God's best.

There are plenty of good things to say yes to, but that doesn't mean they are God's best for you.

Rest. If you do not take care of yourself, no one else will. As women, and working women in particular, we often leave ourselves for last. It's part of our giving, nurturing nature to allow everyone else to butt in line in front of us.

Take time to rest. Time alone. Lock yourself in the bathroom and read a book. Go for a walk. Sit in a coffeehouse alone with a fancy coffee. Do something to take care of you. This goes hand-in-hand with saying no, but is essential if you want to win at work and work wisely for the Lord.

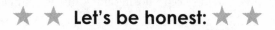

## ★ ★ Let's be honest: ★ ★

*Are you working wisely or wasting time?*
*Do you want to hear God say, "Well done!"?*
*Do you need to learn to say no to the good and yes to God's best?*
*How often do you take time to rest?*

# Work with the Right Motives

One reason there is so much dissatisfaction in work, and lack of engagement in the workplace, is because we often feel like our work doesn't count for something significant.

For the believer, it starts with knowing and believing your work matters to God, that He values your work as a tool in His hand to further His kingdom. Your position in XYZ Company is just as important to God and essential to His work as the pastor on the pulpit and the missionary in the field. It is the reason behind your "something."

Your "something" counts in another profound way: through the eternality of your work.

### *Work done for my glory goes away. Work done for God's glory lasts for eternity.*

Not only does it matter to view your work through God's eyes and to obey His calling to a particular workplace, it also matters if you do your work with the right motives.

In 1 Corinthians 3, we hear about the fire of purification that our work will one day pass through. Every person's work will be shown for what it is. Work built on the foundation of Jesus Christ, according to this passage, will pass through the fire and remain whole, just as precious stones and silver and gold remain intact after going through a fire. All work done for any other reason will burn up like wood or hay. I don't need to tell you how those things fare after going through a fire!

### *Eternal Work always comes down to motivation.*

If the reason for our "something" is anything other than God's glory, it will end up as burnt ash floating in the wind someday. Do you want to work this hard on something only to have it charred to nothing? I don't.

That is why I wrote the phrase "Make your something count for something" on the blackboard by my door. It's a constant reminder of the "why" behind the what. It's a heart check, a motivation check, a smoke detector for my work.

Every day, before you enter your workplace calling, check your motives at the door. Before you put on that nametag or get in the elevator or sit at your desk, ask yourself, "What am I here for?"

Without doing that, you run the risk of spending the next eight or ten hours doing something that won't last.

Do you want all your hard work to go up in a puff of smoke on the day you stand before Christ? Or do you want it to have an impact that lasts forever?

My guess is that no one will say they want their work to count for nothing. And yet, so many God-fearing believers get up every morning and go to work with no thought of what their work means to God, or their motivation for doing it.

 **Let's be honest:**

*What motivates you to go to work?*
*Is your work done for your glory, or God's?*
*Does the truth of your work passing through a fire make you want to change your motivation?*
*After going through the Win at Work section, do you have a new perspective on your work? It's no longer a money-making machine to fill the space of your days. Now it has meaning, purpose, and value beyond a paycheck or position.*
*Can you see now how you can win at work as you shift your perspective from money to people and purpose? Can you see your work the way God does, as a ministry? A ministry to God, yourself, and to others? A ministry to others sounds more like mission work, doesn't it? Exactly.*

CHAPTER EIGHT

# YOUR WORK, YOUR MISSION FIELD

*"I believe that one of the next great moves of God is going to be through the believers in the workplace."*
—Billy Graham

God is great at using one thing for many purposes. He can use your work for both your good and His glory. He can use it to accomplish financial, spiritual, and physical purposes. He can use it to impact your life as well as the lives of others.

I once worked for a custom home designer. She was far from a woman of faith, but instead sought out fulfillment in Eastern religious practices and the worship of self. She was far from the One, True, and Living God I know and love. Yet, God called me to work for her. The two other employees in her company were women of faith as well. All three of us were there at the same time to show and share with her who God was and how He loved her.

Unfortunately, this woman spurned every attempt of God to reach out to her and draw her to a real relationship with Himself. A few years later, God called all three of us out of that company within a few weeks of each other and into new jobs with other employers. I don't know if she ever turned to God after that, but I do know, beyond the shadow of a doubt, God had us all there for a season to reach out to her.

One of the great things about God is that He sees our hearts and He knows our needs. He does this with every human being on the earth. He knows who needs Him in your workplace. He knows who needs to be set free and He wants to use you to bring about His will in the hearts of people with whom you work every day.

You may think it is impossible to share God and your faith in the workplace. That is just another Wonder Woman lie: work is work, and your faith doesn't belong there. But God's truth says:

### It's impossible to leave your faith at home.

Many believers feel they have to leave their faith in God at home, that God is not welcome in their workplace setting.

- Maybe you feel your work culture is devoid of any sense of morality.

- Maybe you are trying to obey the constraints laid out by your HR department so you won't be reprimanded for initiating unacceptable workplace conversations.

- Maybe you are scared of what will happen to you if your faith is known.

- Maybe you've buried your faith up to this point and now you're ashamed to open up and proclaim it.

Whatever the reason, you feel as if the doors of your workplace are locked to God. Let me assure you, nothing could be further from the truth. God is not limited by culture, your HR department, or your own insecurities. God is already with you and in you when you step into the doors of your workplace calling.

**No door is locked to God. God opens doors and makes a way where there is no way.**

Your part is to follow Him, trust Him, and know you are not alone.

"To whom God would make known what is the riches of the glory of this mystery among the Gentiles; which is Christ in you, the hope of glory" (Col. 1:27 [King James Version]).

Isn't it amazing—that God lives within you? Christ also lives within you, the hope of glory. Everywhere you go, God is there. Every place your foot lands brings God to that place. It is impossible to separate yourself from Him.

"Don't you realize that your body is the temple of the Holy Spirit, who lives in you and was given to you by God? You do not belong to yourself" (1 Cor. 6:19 [New Living Translation]).

If we live out the truth of this fact in our daily lives and actions at work, we won't have to start a conversation about God at work. It will be evident to everyone that we belong to Him. God will shine so brightly through us that others will come to us, asking about our God. Our part is to let the light shine. Don't hide it!

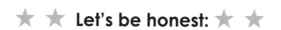

## ★ ★ Let's be honest: ★ ★

*Do you feel like you have to leave your faith at home?*
*Have you buried your faith in your workplace setting until now?*
*How does the knowledge that God accompanies you*
*to work give you boldness?*

# Just Shine!

"You are the light of the world—like a city on a hilltop that cannot be hidden. No one lights a lamp and then puts it under a basket. Instead, a lamp is placed on a stand, where it gives light to everyone in the house. In the same way, let your good deeds shine out for all to see, so that everyone will praise your heavenly Father" (Mt. 5:14–16 [New Living Translation]).

## It is impossible to hide light.

If I turn on a light in a dark room—even a small light—the darkness has to flee. You may be a small light. You may be the only light in your workplace, but you are still a light.

So how do we shine our light? How do we influence our workplace for God? How do we light our calling in the workplace? What does it look like to "shine our light"?

### 1. Get out of God's way.

First of all, notice that we are to "let" or "allow" our light to shine. Let Jesus, the Light of the World, shine through you. Just as John said that Jesus must increase and he must decrease, so too must we put God first and foremost while we place ourselves in the background. It's called humility and it's a beautiful tool of God.

### 2. Live like a child of the King.

When you "go public" with your faith, all eyes will immediately start watching you. Not focusing on what you say, but on what you do. People have met enough "Sunday Christians" and have experienced enough hypocrites to be cynical about those who call themselves Christians. And rightly so.

When your actions actually back up your words, people take notice. You won't have to say a thing. They will see something different—something they lack and something they want.

They will see it . . .

- •. . . in the way you talk to others.

- •. . . in your integrity and honesty when you make a mistake.

- •. . . in how you respond to a complaining customer or demanding boss.

- •. . . in your handling of difficult and tempting situations.

*Be wise in the way you act toward outsiders; make the most of every opportunity. Let your conversation be always full of grace, seasoned with salt, so that you may know how to answer everyone.*

(Col. 4:5–6 [New International Version])

## 3. Be intentional in your relationships.

You may have heard that people don't care how much you know until they know how much you care. Ask God to give you a supernatural amount of love and care for those in your workplace calling (even those who seem unlovable). Only God can do this. This is miraculous love; this is the love that God has for each soul that walks the earth. A love so great that He was willing to let His own Son die for them. That kind of love.

Everyone wants love. Everyone.

When you treat your co-workers as if you actually love and care for them, they will notice. After all, isn't that what God did for you?

How different would our workplaces be if we did this? What kind of internal impact could we have on lost souls if we lived the truth of God within us at work? What would happen if we paused before we opened the doors of our workplace and said, "God, you promised you are with me everywhere I go. You dwell within me and I am bringing you into work today. Shine through me in this place!"

What does it mean to shine?

If you grew up going to church, you've heard this song a million times (my apologies in advance for getting it stuck in your head):

> *This little light of mine, I'm gonna let it shine.*
> *This little light of mine, I'm gonna let it shine.*
> *This little light of mine, I'm gonna let it shine.*
> *Let it shine, let it shine, let it shine.*

Catchy tune, isn't it? Its message and lyrics come from this verse, straight from the lips of Jesus: "In the same way, let your light shine before others, that they may see your good deeds and glorify your Father in heaven" (Mt. 5:16 [New International Version]).

If we are going to follow Jesus's instructions, we need to look a little deeper into the verse.

## THE REASON FOR THE SHINE:

We are not to shine so everyone can see how great we are and how many good deeds we do. We are to shine light on how great God is. When God is the reason behind the works we do and when we shine for the right reason, those around us will see God, instead of us.

## THE PATH OF THE SHINE:

Notice that the command is passive. We are to *let* our light shine, not *make* it shine. A lamp doesn't produce light; it is the electricity flowing through the lamp that causes the light to shine. When we force the shine, it comes off as fake. And people can tell it's fake. Like the noticeable difference between a fluorescent light and beautiful rays of sunshine.

## THE SOURCE OF THE SHINE:

What is this light that we are to let shine? It is the "Light of the World" (Jn. 8:12 [New Living Translation]), "The light that is the light of men," and "the light shines in darkness" (Jn. 1:4–5 [New King James Version]). The source of the shine is none other than Jesus himself. We don't have to create the Light, we just let Jesus shine through us. He is the source; we are the conduit.

## THE SOUND OF THE SHINE:

Have you ever heard the sound that light makes? Neither have I. That's because light makes no sound. It is something you see, not something you hear.

Likewise, letting our light shine is more about what we do than what we say. Let your good works speak for themselves and you won't have to say a word.

If you are open about your faith, good works should flow from your actions. Those who witness your shining light will likely be moved to respond.

## THE RESULT OF THE SHINE:

When we shine in earnest, as laid out in the steps above, the result is beautiful: God gets the glory. He gets noticed instead of us. Isn't that what we want after all? Don't we pray that God would be glorified? Does He deserve anything less than full credit and all the glory?

## ★ ★ Let's be honest: ★ ★

*Does the light of Christ shine through you?*
*If you can shine without saying a word, how will that change your actions?*
*Does your workplace need a good dose of God's light?*

When you shine God's light, people will want to know why you're different. That will give you the opportunity to share your faith at work.

# What if I'm afraid to share my faith at work?

You're in good company. Fear is the reason most people don't share their faith at work.

Not fear of losing your job or breaking some law or getting a bad review from your boss—that's only part of it. The root fear is the fear of others not liking us. We all have a desire to be accepted. We want approval from those around us. It's part of our nature of wanting to belong.

As believers, we are not called to belong or win a popularity contest. We are, however, called to share the truth. And if we don't share the truth that sets people free in our workplace, who will?

In the verse known as the Great Commission, Jesus said these words to His disciples,

"And then he told them, 'Go into all the world and preach the Good News to everyone'" (Mk. 16:15 [New Living Translation]).

We often associate this verse with missionaries and pastors, but this verse applies to every believer.

The original language of that verse reads like this: "As you are going into the world, preach the gospel." As you are going. In other words, as you go about your life from day to day—at work, at the store, in the airport—share as you go. Jesus didn't place any limitations on this call, neither by profession, position, or place.

Are you treated differently at your work because you are a believer? Are you ostracized in your workplace environment because you call yourself a Christian?

Take heart, because you are in good company.

Jesus told His disciples that the servant is not greater than the Master. Since Jesus was persecuted to the point of death, we can naturally expect some type of persecution for being His followers.

There are a thousand stories of persecution of believers through the ages, stories that are still unraveling today in many parts of the world. Most of the stories you hear involve people who are martyred for their faith or imprisoned by governments for sharing God's Word. But there are also countless stories that we have not heard of people who are ridiculed, scorned, and alienated for their faith.

All are forms of persecution. All seek to discourage people from sharing their faith. All will continue to happen until Christ returns or calls us home.

If you are reading this and live in America, chances are pretty good any persecution you face is not life threatening. Someone might tease you or avoid you. It's persecution, yes, but you probably won't die from it. You are not staring in the face of death or imprisonment, right?

And yet, that co-worker, boss, customer, vendor is facing eternal judgment with no hope of release.

I say all this to my shame, as well. The idea of feeling awkward or uncomfortable can be enough to silence my own testimony in the workplace sometimes.

How do I share my faith, then? Here are a few introductory ways to share your faith in the workplace that may help you break through the fear:

## 1. Ask to pray for them:

Our co-workers often end up sharing their personal struggles or tragedies with us. After all, we all spend a lot of time together throughout the week. Whenever someone shares a burden with me, I ask if I can pray for them. No one has ever turned down an offer for prayer. When people are going through hard times, they often turn their thoughts toward the things of God (or at least some higher power). This provides us an opportunity, an open door to step through.

Sometimes I even offer to pray for them on the spot, if they are comfortable with it.

Follow up and ask them if they have seen an answer to prayer yet. This will give you more opportunities to share with them.

## 2. Share your God stories:

Everyone has a story of how God brought them to their place of faith in Jesus. Sharing your story of spiritual transformation is a powerful thing. When we are real and honest about our past sins and God's healing power, it is hard for others to ignore the reality of God.

Share stories about answers to prayer, or ways you have seen God move in your life and in the lives of your family. Many people don't believe God answers prayer. When you share how God answered yours, it piques their interest.

## 3. Live it first:

When people see you walk the walk, instead of just talking the talk, they will sit up and take notice. I know I said this before, but it bears repeating. An authentic life in Christ always makes others notice the difference. After watching you and your life for months, or even years, curiosity will overtake them and they will want to know why you are so different. Which is when you go back to my second point and share your story.

These are just a few tips to help you get started, but the number one obstacle to sharing your faith in the workplace will always be you, and your fears.

## Let's be honest:

*What would you do if you weren't afraid?*
*Who would you reach out to if fear wasn't a factor?*
*What person in your workplace calling just came into your mind as you were reading through this?*

If you do share with that person and they steer clear of you for a while, or get mad at you, will it deter you from continuing to share with others? Or will you instead think about all that Jesus, and others, has suffered in the way of persecution and consider yourself in good company?

As you go, share.

### Squash the fear and share the love of God with someone.

They need it more than you may know.

You may not need to share all by yourself. The great thing about God's people is that they're everywhere.

## There's more of us than you think.

They are in the cubicle or register next to you.
They ride in the elevator beside you.
They eat in your breakroom with you.

How many of the people you see every day are believers? How many of them are trying to live out their faith day to day? How many of them believe and feel as passionate about God as you do?

Can you count them? Can you name them?

It may surprise you to learn that there are more of them than you think, more of us.

If you work for a large corporation, you may be somewhat limited in what you can share about your faith in the workplace. Maybe there isn't a formal policy, but you are afraid that being honest and vocal about your faith will result in you getting fired or ostracized by your co-workers.

But what if that person next to you is a believer who is more afraid than you are? What if one bold statement from you would encourage them to share their beliefs and desire for God in their life with you?

One thing I have discovered through my years in the workplace is I am not as alone in my faith/work walk as I once thought I was.

When Elijah was hiding from Jezebel in a cave in the middle of nowhere, he complained to God about being the only prophet left who would stand up against the tyranny of the unbelieving King of the day (1 Kings 19).

What did God say to Elijah as he hid in that cave claiming to be the only one?

"No! I have seven thousand others who have not bowed a knee to Baal" (Rom. 11:4 [New Living Translation]).

God was telling Elijah, in no uncertain terms, that he was not alone. There were plenty of other dedicated believers just like him all around the land.

Elijah was certain that he was the only one who still cared about God and the things of God, but Elijah was wrong. God knew the truth.

•God still knows the truth today.

•God knows the exact location of every believer in the world today.

•God knows those who are His.

•Can I encourage you today by telling you the same is true for your workplace?

•You are not the only one.

•God knows who is there with you.

•God knows those who are His.

Ask God to show you, to give you the courage to say something about Him in your work environment as you wait in line or ride the elevator. See if you ignite a spark, a smile, a knowing nod.

That spark or nod could turn into your best ally and partner in faith in your workplace. Don't just look for those who are like you or belong to the same denomination. That doesn't matter to God; what matters is what is on the inside, the reality of a relationship with God through Jesus Christ.

Many believers are walking around as secret agents, afraid of offending someone, not feeling confident to share their faith or reach out. You are not alone in your silence.

Now, more than ever, we need to be bold in our faith; we need to live out loud in the workplace and every area of our lives. Be on the lookout for others who believe in your workplace. Partner with them to bring God's light, love, and grace to your company and co-workers.

## ★ ★ Let's be honest: ★ ★

*How many believers are in your workplace?*
*What small step can you take to find out who is?*
*How has boldness from another believer given you boldness?*

People all around you are searching for the truth and you have the truth. Do not withhold it from them, even if they seem like a lost cause.

## Who is the "lost cause" in your workplace?

The musty scent of the dank prison cell stings his nostrils. His wrists and ankles now bleed where the shackles cut into his raw, filth-ridden skin. Left to rot. A lost cause.

He's sure he hasn't eaten for at least a day or maybe more, but somehow, in this moment, he isn't hungry anymore.

He's singing.

Not a low, woeful song of his sufferings. He is singing a song of praise to God. Praise in prison. His cellmate joins in, and now emboldened by the duet they both raise their voices louder and louder. There is no need to sing on key; they just want everyone in the prison to know the greatness of their God.

The vocalist? Paul, the apostle. His backup singer? Silas. Now the story sounds more familiar, right? (Acts 16:25–34)

What does this have to do with your co-workers? Everything.

You know this true story of Paul and Silas and how, while in prison, they sang and praised God at midnight. But let's back up for a second and remember who Paul was before he became one of the top apostles. In his BC (before Christ) days, Paul was Saul. A persecutor of believers, hell-bent on destroying the early church.

If you conducted a survey in the early church and asked who would be the most unlikely person to become a believer and follower of Jesus, 99.9 percent of those surveyed would have said Saul the Pharisee. He didn't just ignore or ridicule believers, he had them arrested and imprisoned. He traveled from town to town to gather up as many "Jesus Freaks" as he could and lock them up. He had plenty of support for his zealous endeavors as well. Every believer in the early church had probably written off Saul as a lost cause.

## No one is a lost cause to God.

Who have you written off?

No one in a million years would've guessed this man who hated and even supported the death of these "little Christs" would become one of them!

Who in your workplace is the least likely to come to Christ? Who opposes your beliefs with vehemence, maybe even goes out of their way to torment you for your faith? Who would you say is a long shot? A lost cause? Who have you written off?

I wonder who taught Paul (Saul) to praise God in prison. Scripture doesn't say, but I can only wonder if Saul (Paul) had heard the same kind of worship session from believers after he locked them up and threw away the key. Paul tried to lock up Christ (in essence), but he still couldn't get away from the truth.

Your co-worker can't get away from the truth as long as you're around. Which is why they often try to get rid of you, trip you up, or get you in trouble with HR.

Maybe that "lost cause" is the person God is still calling out of the darkness and into His marvelous light. Maybe that co-worker you've written off is the next "Paul."

Who have you quit praying for?

No one was praying for Saul to get saved. At least, not that we are aware. They were all busy trying to avoid him. In fact, after Paul's blinding conversion, God tells a believer named Ananias to go pray for him, to bring about healing for Saul's (Paul's) blindness. Ananias obeys, but he only agrees to go after God tells him that Saul (Paul) will suffer for him (Acts 9:10–19).

"Suffer, you say? Okay, then I'll go pray for him, but only if he's going to suffer big time!"

Can you relate? Is there someone in your workplace who you would rather see get a dose of God's wrath instead of His mercy? That's the one to start praying for again. That's the one whose dirty soul needs your help to find God's healing.

Who avoids you?

After his conversion, Paul avoided the believers in Jerusalem, the main hub of Christianity at the time. He went off to the desert for three years to have his mind renewed. He wasn't running from God, but he didn't feel comfortable going to church quite yet.

Is there someone like that in your office? Maybe they have professed to be a believer, but don't live like it. Maybe they haven't written off God, but they aren't ready to be "all in" yet. Maybe they avoid you because they feel the sting of conviction. Maybe they avoid you because they are afraid of surrender. Maybe they feel like there's no mercy for them because they know to do right, but aren't doing it. Maybe you look at them as a lost cause too.

Make sure no one is avoiding you because you have become one of those annoying, in-your-face people who offer more condemnation than grace. Going around quoting scripture all the time and condemning everyone will cause people to avoid you (check your heart if that one stung you).

If that's not the reason for the avoidance, don't write them off. They are one that the Father sees and runs to while they are still a long way off. He leaves the ninety-nine righteous to chase after one lost sheep. God is so excited to see his sheep coming. Are you?

This is not a scathing rebuke, but rather a wake-up call to all us believers in the marketplace today.

### *We need to start viewing the people in our workplace the way God views them.*

- God loves every person in your workplace.
- God has not written off any of your co-workers.
- God wants to use you to reach them.

## ★ ★ Let's be honest: ★ ★

*Who is the lost cause in your workplace?*

*Who have you quit praying for?*

*Are you ready to be a part of someone's redemption story*

*like Ananias in Paul's?*

*Are you ready to sing praises in the captivity of your Christ-hostile workplace?*

*Are you ready to love and pray for those you work with every day?*

It's time.

## Be the Best Employee Ever

See the importance and possibilities in treating your work as your mission field? Up until now, it's been more about an attitude shift than an action list. Let's look at where the rubber meets the road and discover some action steps for boldness to share the truth that sets free.

The first and most important step is to be an outstanding employee or boss. You can't be slacking off at work and trying to share your faith. It doesn't jive.

God desires us to be the best at what we do because we are His ambassadors here on earth.

An ambassador to another country is there to give an accurate and honest representation of their home country and seek to build relationships between the two nations. The same is true for us. As Ambassadors for Christ in our workplaces we must represent Him with accuracy and honesty. We should seek to build relationships between our co-workers and Christ.

How do we do this?

As in all things in our lives, God's Word gives us the direction and clarity we need to accomplish the task He asks us to do.

Ephesians 6 is a chapter on relationships—relationships between children and parents, husbands and wives, employees and bosses. Here's the part that applies to employees and bosses:

> *Slaves, obey your earthly masters with deep respect and fear. Serve them sincerely as you would serve Christ. Try to please them all the time, not just when they are watching you. As slaves of Christ, do the will of God with all your heart. Work with enthusiasm, as though you were working for the Lord rather than for people. Remember that the Lord will reward each one of us for the good we do, whether we are slaves or free.*
>
> *Masters, treat your slaves in the same way. Don't threaten them; remember, you both have the same Master in heaven, and he has no favorites.*

(Eph. 6:5–9 [New Living Translation]).

We are not slaves and masters, but we are employees and bosses (which often feels like a slave/master arrangement).

Being the best employee or boss boils down to three main things: activity, attitude, and awareness.

## ACTIVITY

The activity that sets us apart as Christians in the workplace is obedience. Our obedience to our bosses shows that we honor their position and the authority that God has placed over us. Obedience doesn't mean that we agree with every decision our boss makes. It doesn't mean we endorse every action that they take. We obey because God commands us to (disclaimer: God does not require us to obey directives that go against other areas of scripture or are against the law. We'll touch on that in the next chapter).

As employees, we are obliged (and paid) to follow direction from our superiors. Obedience lightens the load of our bosses. It makes us a joy to have around, instead of a pain.

Serve your boss as you would serve Christ. Sound impossible? Not if you have the right attitude and remember that Christ is your true boss.

## ATTITUDE

God wants us to have a sincere and pleasing attitude. An attitude of doing good work all the time, instead of just when the boss is watching, can set us apart from unbelieving co-workers. If we only work hard when the boss is watching, we are no different from our co-workers. Jesus said we are the salt of the earth and the light of the world (Mt. 5:13–16), but nothing sets us apart as salt and light in the workplace if we do our work with the same attitude as everyone else. The attitude of "less is more" should not be present in the believer and can actually turn our bosses away from God, instead of toward Him.

## AWARENESS

Where Christians have the biggest impact in their workplace is having a keen awareness of who they work for (just a friendly reminder).

When we are aware that God is our boss, our work becomes the best, since we are working for the BEST BOSS ever. We are motivated by the knowledge that we will eventually be rewarded by God Himself for our hard work. This awareness also frees us from the traps of comparison, competition, and other office politics.

How does this apply to bosses? The last few verses state that bosses should treat their employees the same way, without threatening them or showing favoritism. The directives and application are pretty clear. We are to be the best employees and bosses, no matter the job that God has called us to do.

Is it clear and simple? Yes. Is it always easy? No.

**God never asks us to do something without giving us the power to do it.**

God asks us to be the best employee and boss because He knows our positive influence can lead others into a relationship with Him. He asks us because we are His ambassadors here on earth and He wants us to represent Him well. In addition to asking us, He empowers us.

God asks you to be the best, because He has the power to help you be the best.

Are you going to make mistakes? You bet! But that is where God's grace comes into play. We repent, He forgives, and then He helps us to do it right the next time.

## ★ ★ Let's be honest: ★ ★

*Are you the best employee/boss your company has?*
*Do you represent Christ well?*

Do an attitude check on your work.

# More ways to be a standout for God

Being a standout for God in your workplace is hard, but not impossible. You have probably heard the saying, "Preach the Gospel at all times and, when necessary, use your words."

Our actions always speak louder than our words. You can tell your whole office that you are a Christian. You can have a Bible on your desk and verses on your wall, but if you don't live and work differently than nonbelievers, no one will take notice of your God.

Many workplaces don't allow, or frown upon, people sharing religion in the office. You may find it difficult to say anything about

God in words, but you can let your actions speak volumes about Him every day.

Here are five practical ways that you can be a standout and get God noticed in your workplace calling:

**1. Adopt a "student attitude" in the workplace:**

Finishing a degree or training course doesn't mean you've finished learning. While attending classes in your major coursework, your attitude is to learn something you can use in the workplace. You're excited about the knowledge you gain and anticipate the time when you can finally put it to good use.

Jesus's disciples had an attitude of learning. They hungered for His wisdom and knowledge. Mary of Bethany sat at the feet of Jesus, hanging on His every word. She wanted to learn more (Lk. 10:39).

Come to work each day with that same attitude. If you come to your workplace expecting to learn something new that will help you in your job, you will. You don't know it all yet.

- Study your company, your industry, and your company's products and services.

- Study the competition.

- Ask questions.

- Accept help from others.

- Don't be afraid to admit you don't know something.

You will be miles ahead of many of your co-workers who have been there for years and your enthusiasm for learning won't go unnoticed. When you don't try to be the office "know it all," your humility and willingness to learn will stand out.

## 2. Show up on time:

Things happen. Cars break down, weather and traffic mess with your schedule, you spill coffee on yourself. Delays will inevitably occur. Don't make tardiness a habit. Show up early; there is no such thing as "fashionably late" in the workplace.

When you come late to everything, you are telling others that your time is more important than theirs. It's disrespectful and unnecessary.

This may seem rudimentary, but I'm amazed how many adults don't grasp this concept, even when they have been in the workplace for decades. When you show up on time—or even early—for work, appointments with clients, and meetings, you will stand out above the pack.

Showing this kind of respect toward others in your workplace calling places value upon them, and everyone likes to feel valued.

## 3. Let others know you care:

You don't have to be "Dr. Phil" for your office (nor should you), but you should make a point to be kind, honest, and caring with everyone you meet through work. It's not about the sales, the metrics, and the deadlines; it's about the people. It's always about the people. Ask people how they are doing (and mean it!). Get to know about their families, their hobbies, and about them, as a person.

You will not be able to share God's love and story of redemption with your co-workers if you never treat them with kindness. Kindness and decency are vanishing in our society and in our world as a whole.

You don't have to like everyone you come into contact with, but you have a direct obligation from God to love others. There are always going to be co-workers who rub you the wrong way. There will be screaming irate customers, demanding bosses, and backbiting co-workers.

Showing kindness and caring about people, regardless of their behavior, will help you stand out as different and will open doors for further conversation and sharing about God. Let people vent to you. Offer to pray for them. Pray for them without offering it. You will stand out and God will get noticed.

### 4. Do your best every day:

God doesn't expect perfection and neither should you. But you can bring your best. Every day. When you do the best with what God has given you, you will find great satisfaction in your work.

When you are able to leave your workplace knowing every day that you did the best you could, you will never have an issue with work-life balance. You will have job satisfaction and God will get the glory.

### 5. You will have great successes and make great mistakes. Be humble in both:

Sometimes you are going to nail it. Sometimes you are going to tank. That's just life. Whether you succeed or fail, remember to be humble. You owe some of your successes to others, so don't take the credit for them as if you were flying solo.

And, when you blow it, don't include anyone except yourself in the blame. Finger-pointing is just an excuse. Take the rap for something that wasn't completely your fault. It shows maturity. It shows that you understand that the world doesn't revolve around you. And that's a good thing to understand.

Share your successes; own your failures. Not only will you stand out from the crowd, others will also want to work with you in the future.

These steps aren't rocket science; you don't need a degree to be a standout. It's always a matter of choice. Choose to be a standout and you will. Your actions will speak loud and clear and those actions will open the door for you to use your words to share the Good News with those around you.

God calls us to be different. Scripture calls us a "peculiar people" or special. When we act differently, others will notice a difference and want to know why. When they start asking "why" we're different, we can introduce them to the One who makes all the difference: Jesus.

This is not an exhaustive list. But it will get you started in standing out so that you earn the right to speak truth into the lives of those in your workplace.

### ★ ★ Let's be honest: ★ ★

*Which of the five ways to be a standout do you need to work on?*
*Do you sit at the feet of Jesus and learn from Him like Mary did?*
*How can learning from Jesus help you be a standout in your workplace?*

# Nothing broadcasts your faith quite like love.

Another key to living out loud, or broadcasting your faith in your work (your mission field), is simple but effective. There is one thing that is more powerful than any book or tool out there on how to share your faith, and it's found in this verse: "Your love for one another will prove to the world that you are my disciples" (Jn. 13:35 [New Living Translation]).

As believers and disciples of Jesus, we are often hardest on those within the faith. We forget that we are all on the same team. In this verse, Jesus lays out to his disciples the one thing that will make them instantly recognizable as His own: their love for one another.

We can quote whole chapters of the Bible, but if we don't have love for one another, our words will have no impact. We can live holy, upright lives, but if we speak ill of our fellow Christians, no one will pay attention to how we live. We can talk all day long about God's love and grace, but if we do not have the same love and grace for our brothers and sisters in Christ, no one will believe in God's love.

Does it matter what church you attend, the style of worship music you approve, or which version of scripture you read?

No. What matters is your love for each other. Nothing speaks louder to the unbelieving world than the pure, unconditional love that believers have for each other. You know what else speaks loudly? When we fight and debate with fellow believers in front of a watching world. Stop it.

### Remember, we are all on the same team. God's team.

Jesus picked each of us, just as He picked each of the disciples. Each of us is uniquely made and lovingly chosen. God designed each believer to be a part of the larger body of Christ. God chose each of us to come together to display God and His plan for the church as a whole.

We were never meant to be solo Christians, operating independently of one another. Rather, we are called upon to live as complete, redeemed brides of Christ. When unbelievers see us fighting with each other, they will want nothing to do with our God. When unbelievers see us fractured and feuding, they will steer clear of our churches, our gospel, and our Lord.

It's time we heed the words of Jesus and let the whole world know we are His disciples. The only way to do that is through love. Your challenge is to broadcast your faith through love. Love for the unbeliever, yes, but even more through love for one another.

### ★ ★ Let's be honest: ★ ★

*Do you find it hard to love*
*your fellow brothers and sisters in Christ sometimes?*
*Do you divide the body of Christ arguing over things that don't matter?*
*How can you show real love for another believer?*

## What Living Out Loud Is NOT

You have the foundations for living your work, your mission field, and living your faith out loud. Let's look at the opposite of living out loud.

I asked the women I surveyed what help they needed in their workplace calling. The majority of them answered: "How to share my faith at work."

In other words: "How can I lead others to the beautiful reality of Jesus without being that annoying person that everyone wants to avoid?"

**1. Living out loud is not about words**

If we tout the love of God, but treat others with hate, we have not only missed the mark, we may also be keeping others from finding freedom in the truth. We can talk all day long about Jesus and God's gift of forgiveness, but if we don't live out that truth, the message gets lost.

Focus your actions on being Christ-like instead of talking about Christ.

### 2. Living out loud is not about feelings

It really doesn't matter if you feel godly or feel worthy or feel like you can be a witness in your workplace. Living out loud is not about feeling worthy to share the message.

You will never feel worthy enough to share the incredible message of God's grace. None of us are worthy. For some crazy reason, God thought it would be best to use us to spread the message of hope.

> **It doesn't matter how you feel because God is bigger than your feelings.**

- •God can overcome your feelings of inadequacy.
- •God can overcome your feelings of guilt for saying or doing the wrong thing.
- •God can overcome your feelings of you.

See, it's not about you. It's not about you being the Billy Graham of your workplace. It's supposed to be about Jesus. About God's gift of grace and mercy. About forgiveness for mistakes and shortcomings.

Focus on who God is instead of how you feel.

### 3. Living out loud is not about being perfect

The truth is, you are going to mess up. You will quote the wrong verse; you will get mad when you should be forgiving. You will make mistakes.

Be real. Own your mistakes and failures with your co-workers. If you want to reach them, they need to see grace in action. That means having grace for yourself. Own your mistakes and shortcomings. The humility you present when you are authentic about your faults will go much farther than putting on a façade of perfection.

**Only God is perfect; the rest of us need His grace.**

Get comfortable with the reality that you will mess up when it comes to sharing your faith in the workplace. Yet, also be confident God can make up for those mistakes.

When I get to share the good news of Jesus with others I pray, "God, please let them remember the good things I said and forget the bad."

God the Holy Spirit influences the heart more than our words or actions do. He is capable of taking up the slack for you, so let Him. Focus on God's ability over your inability.

##  Let's be honest:

*Does the fear of saying the wrong thing hold you back
from sharing your faith?
Do your feelings get in the way of living out loud?
Do you think you need to be perfect in your walk with God
before you can share truth with others?*

Now that you know what *not* to do, here are some final practical steps for sharing your faith in your workplace.

# Pray

There is no better place to start than on your knees. When we seek to start to share our faith in the workplace, we must remember that nothing will happen without prayer.

•Prayer moves the hand that moves the world.

•Prayer moves the Holy Spirit to soften the heart before you even show up for work.

•Prayer is the power behind the message.

If you are feeling unsure of how to share your faith, live out loud, and have an eternal impact in the "mission field" that God has placed you in, you must start with prayer.

## Prayer is the most powerful tool we have.

Often it sits in the shed of our life, unused and collecting dust and spider webs. We pull it out in emergencies (like a chainsaw clearing up the fallen trees in our lives). We may even use it to "prune" our lives occasionally, praying for family and friends.

When is the last time you used prayer in your workplace calling? This is key to your work being your mission field.

Our workplaces can be messy. It's easier to complain about all of the things that are wrong than it is to pray.

•Prayer takes work.

•Prayer takes faith.

•Prayer takes time.

God says in His word, "And we are confident that he hears us whenever we ask for anything that pleases him. And since we know he hears us when we make our requests, we also know that he will give us what we ask for" (1 Jn. 5:14–15 [New Living Translation]).

There is confidence in the power tool of prayer. Confidence not in us, or our abilities, but in the abilities of an Almighty God.

*"Prayer is a mighty instrument, not for getting man's will done in Heaven, but for getting God's will done on earth." —Robert Law*

Your prayers to God to make your boss less demanding or to get rid of an annoying co-worker will probably go unanswered. Those prayers do not have the right motivation behind them. We shouldn't use prayer as a tool to get our own way, but as an agent of change, a catalyst.

What would our lives look like if we used it every day, all day? What kind of change could take place in our workplace calling if we actually used this amazing, powerful tool that is one of our benefits of being a child of God?

Jesus said, "You can pray for anything, and if you have faith, you will receive it" (Mt. 21:22 [New Living Translation]).

Do you believe that verse? If God's Word is true, then you can pray for anything in your workplace and receive it. I have prayed for:

- Safety for employees

- Machines that aren't working right

- Increased sales

- Individual hearts

- Meeting outcomes

Through prayer I have seen amazing, powerful miracles take place. Seeing prayers answered has increased my faith and my influence in the place where God has called me to work.

Maybe you are thinking, "I barely have time to pray for my family and myself. How will I find time to pray for my workplace as well?"

You know that commute time you dread? Perfect time to pray (as a side note: prayer during commuting also helps treat road rage symptoms!). You could arrive five minutes early and pray over your workplace. Pray during meetings and on phone calls; pray during your break or on your way into the building. There's no need to get on your knees, close your eyes, and spend hours in prayer.

I will promise you right here and now, that if you use this tool—this power tool that God has given you in your workplace calling—you will see results!

The results may not happen right away. They may not come in ways you think they should. In some cases, the results may show up in changes in you. But there will be results.

  **Let's be honest:**

*Do you believe prayer is a powerful tool?*
*When is the last time you prayed for your workplace?*
*Will you make a commitment with me to spend the next thirty days praying for your workplace and the people in it?*

Try it for one month and, if you don't see results, you can quit. But you won't want to quit after a month because God keeps His word and you'll start seeing answers to your prayers.

# Know

Before you can introduce God into someone's life, you need to know them. I'm not saying God doesn't give us opportunity to talk to strangers about Him. Of course He does. But when it comes to the workplace, you must start by investing time to get to know the person you are reaching out to.

- Ask questions about their life, their family, and their background.

- Take a genuine interest in their struggles and victories.

- Listen more than you talk.

Taking time to get to know someone in your workplace shows you care, that you aren't just trying to make a convert and move on. In essence, sharing your faith is sharing the relationship you have with God.

**God's plan is all about relationships, not religion.**

Developing a relationship with the people in your workplace lays the groundwork you'll build upon further down the road.

# Respect

No one has ever come to Christ because a believer insulted their current religious beliefs. Respecting other people's religion goes a long way toward building a bridge to sharing your faith. You don't need to agree with their beliefs about God, but you don't need to bash them either. Doing so causes you to lose respect with the people you are trying to reach. Instead:

- Get to know what they believe and why.

- Show interest and respect for what they hold dear.

- Realize that it is all they have ever known and it's important to them.

# Serve

By serving others, you serve God. In serving others and putting their needs before your own, you mimic Jesus's style of evangelism. Serving those you are trying to reach puts your actions before your words.

- Serving others demonstrates that your faith isn't just lip service.

- Serving others displays the heart that God has for them.

- Serving others softens your heart toward their needs.

Find ways to show the tangible love of God to others by serving them. Be "Jesus with skin on" to someone in your workplace and they will listen when you talk about your faith with them.

# Tell

We all have a faith story. Tell yours. When you tell the story of how you came to faith in Jesus, you reveal your own frailty and need. Your story is unique to you. No two believers have the same faith story. Tell yours. Recount the miracle of salvation and the impact of God in your own life. If you have done all the other things listed above, you will have a captive audience.

•Sharing your story reveals your humanity.

•Sharing your story reveals God's grace.

•Sharing your story reveals their need.

You don't need to quote chapter and verse of the plan of salvation. Just tell your story in a conversational way: where you were before you met God, how you met God, and how meeting God changed your life. Nothing fancy or elaborate is necessary. Instead, practice humility.

# Be Humble

Part of humility includes resisting the urge to constantly correct others. Most people who don't have a relationship with God know little about Him and His word. If you have an opportunity to share with someone in your workplace, don't go into how the Levitical sacrifices are a picture of Christ, or how everyone in the world is wrong. They will shut you out quicker than you can say, "Lickety-split."

What they need to hear about is God's love. They need to see God's love in you, not your "rightness." I get it. I have this thing about being right. And so do you.

We all like to be right, even if we don't like to admit it. There's a feeling of satisfaction in being right. You give the knowing smile, you stand a little taller, the chest puffs out, and pride takes over.

But in order for us to be right, it means someone else has to be wrong. How many of us like to be wrong? Anyone?

No one likes to be wrong. No one.

Which is why we have so much war and murder and hatred in our world. Have you ever noticed how when someone is wrong they will go out of their way to prove they are right?

I see that a lot in Christianity. We spend way too much time and energy on "being right" by showing how everyone else is wrong. What if we spent that energy being Jesus to people instead?

## *"Don't be right, be Jesus." —Bob Goff*

Loving like Jesus means we don't have to be right or wrong, we can just love.

One of the great things about following God is that we, as humans, don't have to be right. God is the only source of truth. Sadly, many believers do plenty to skew, twist, and mess up that truth to fit their own agendas.

Let's stop trying so hard to be right and just be Jesus instead.

You may need a refresher course in Jesus. If so, read through the gospels a little every day this week. Learn more about Jesus and mimic Him throughout the week. See if your desire to be right diminishes as you desire to be just like Jesus.

Look at the way Jesus treated people who needed Him. He didn't beat them over the head with the Torah. He met them wherever they were. He gave them truth that would set them free.

Every time you feel like being right, be Jesus instead. Instead of pushing your agenda, push His. Instead of pointing out how someone else is wrong, point out how they are loved.

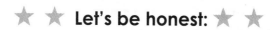

## ★ ★ Let's be honest: ★ ★

*How much time have you spent really getting to know your co-workers?*

*Is there one person you could share your story with this week?*

*Is it more important to you to be right, or be Jesus?*

# Think Like a Farmer

Farmers know something we would do well to learn as we share our faith in the workplace: there's a time to plant, a time to water, and a time to harvest.

Part of your workplace calling purpose is to share God's love with others around you. Fellow employees, customers, bosses, and vendors—they all need Jesus. But you will not see everyone in your workplace come to Christ. You are there to plant and water and sometimes even harvest. God alone provides the yield. He causes the seed of faith that you plant in someone's life to germinate. Then He sends you, or someone else, to water the seed. If you plant and water, there will be a harvest.

Do not try to force someone to believe what you believe or condemn their lifestyle choices. Instead, shine the light, love, and mercy of God into someone's life.

"It's not important who does the planting, or who does the watering. What's important is that God makes the seed grow" (1 Cor. 3:7 [New Living Translation]).

I was having a business phone meeting with a sales rep for a freight company. We were discussing and resolving an issue at hand. After the resolution, I asked if he had an opportunity to hunt yet that year. He began telling me about hunting and how he feels as if he spends so much of his time working that he doesn't get to do the things he would like, including spend more time with his family. "I can't find that balance," he said. You could hear the anguish and depression in his voice.

This opened the door for me to share with him my philosophy that work-life balance is a myth and how it is actually about "center." I shared how God was the center and everything flowed out from that relationship into all the areas of my life. I suggested he find his center. Seed planted!

God brought that situation into my workday. I was there for a reason. That man thanked me for bringing that up. He asked if he could use that analogy. He found some encouragement for his day. I trust God will give me opportunities to water that seed too. I trust God to ultimately make the seed grow into a fruitful relationship with Him.

### If you plant God's seeds, there will someday be a soul harvest.

The thing about gardening is that I cannot plant corn one day and eat it the next. It takes time and patience—two things that I often lack. But God promises that there will be a harvest if we don't give up.

"Let us not become weary in doing good, for at the proper time we will reap a harvest if we do not give up" (Gal. 6:9 [New International Version]).

When I plant that corn in my garden, I can count on a harvest someday (assuming the conditions are right). These are elementary concepts when it comes to gardening, but they apply to our lives as well. We may only plant and water, but God chooses to give the harvest to another. Or, you may witness a harvest that came about from others planting and watering seeds. That's okay. We're all on the same team, remember?

Just because you don't see a co-worker turn their life over to God while you work with them, doesn't mean you haven't made a difference. Don't lose heart. Don't give up hope. Keep on sowing. Keep on watering. Take care of the sowing; God will take care of the growing.

We've discussed your work, your ministry and your work, your mission field. Now we'll look at your work, your minefield.

# CHAPTER NINE

# YOUR WORK, YOUR MINEFIELD

Work can be like a minefield. We take a bunch of imperfect human beings with different backgrounds, personalities, and abilities. Then, we put them in one place and try to get them to accomplish the same goal. Sounds like a recipe for disaster to me!

Working women of faith must sometimes navigate around mines as we try to do our work God's way. The mines are numerous and stepping on one could end in disaster. To win at work, we need to equip ourselves to navigate these mines (issues) in a way that aligns with our faith and our purpose, as women who have been set free.

When I asked working women of faith which issues (mines) they encounter at work, here's what they said:

**Workplace drama  73%**
**Asked to do something against your beliefs  23%**
**Persecution for your faith  14%**
**Sexual harassment  13%**
**Discrimination  11%**
**Romantic temptations  8%**
**Asked to do something illegal  7%**

(Multiple answers allowed)

Can you relate? Have you experienced any of these mines in your work? How can you respond in a way that helps you win at work?

We often look to a spouse, a friend, or the internet for answers to day-to-day workplace issues, instead of turning first to the One who has all the answers: God.

God said it Himself, "His divine power has given us everything we need for a godly life through our knowledge of him who called us by his own glory and goodness" (2 Pet. 1:3 [New International Version]).

That means that by His divine power (which has no equal), we already have everything we need to emulate God at work, at home, and in every place and situation.

God's Word tells us how to respond by the truth of His Word. That's how we'll approach these issues (mines) for guidance in the workplace.

# Workplace Drama

Since this one was a big mine for the women I surveyed, we're going to park here for a little bit and tackle it.

## WORKPLACE DRAMA, THE ROOT CAUSE

Workplace drama is a real issue and a huge problem. I dare say everyone has had to deal with it at some point in their workplace calling.

The first thing to help you face this issue in your workplace calling is to have the right perspective about human nature. You work with human beings, and human beings are sinful creatures. Romans 3 does a great job of describing the sinful state of mankind:

"As the Scriptures say, 'No one is righteous—not even one. No one is truly wise; no one is seeking God. All have turned away; all have become useless. No one does good, not a single one. Their talk is foul, like the stench from an open grave. Their tongues are filled with lies. Snake venom drips from their lips. Their mouths are full of cursing and bitterness. They rush to commit murder. Destruction and misery always follow them. They don't know where to find peace. They have no fear of God at all'" (Rom. 3:10–18 [New Living Translation]).

Sound like anyone you work with? Your co-workers—the ones creating and perpetuating all the drama in your workplace? They are sinners, plain and simple.

"For all have sinned, and come short of the glory of God" (Rom. 3:23 [King James Version]).

Understanding the nature of mankind will help you understand the true source of workplace drama.

All you have to do is go back to the beginning to find the first evidence. Adam and Eve had the job of taking care of the Garden of Eden. God gave Adam strict instructions on what he and Eve could and could not eat in the garden (Gen. 3).

Eve listened to the deceitful lies of satan and ate the forbidden fruit, offering it next to Adam, who also ate it. When they realized their sin, they tried to hide it. Once God brought it out in the open, they immediately started the blame game. They did whatever they could to avoid responsibility for their own actions. This same sin is at the root of all workplace drama.

### The only cure for sin is the cross.

Reading further in Romans 3 we can see this solution:

"Yet God, with undeserved kindness, declares that we are righteous. He did this through Christ Jesus when he freed us from the penalty for our sins. For God presented Jesus as the sacrifice for sin.

People are made right with God when they believe that Jesus sacrificed his life, shedding his blood. This sacrifice shows that God was being fair when he held back and did not punish those who sinned in times past, for he was looking ahead and including them in what he would do in this present time.

"God did this to demonstrate his righteousness, for he himself is fair and just, and he declares sinners to be right in his sight when they believe in Jesus" (Rom. 3:24–26 [New Living Translation]).

If the only solution to sin is the cross, and the source of workplace drama is sin, then the only real solution is Jesus.

### Pray for your co-workers who create workplace drama.

Pray for their salvation; pray for yourself to have patience; pray that God's Spirit will keep you from participating.

What steps must we take first to deal with workplace drama?

•Realize the source is sin.

•Recognize the solution is the cross.

•Release the sinner to God.

This isn't to say that you are somehow better than those who do not know Christ. It is a realization you only have one enemy and it's not the office drama queen. Our only enemy is satan. Just as he worked to deceive Adam and Eve, he is working today to deceive us and those around us.

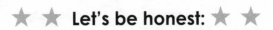

## Let's be honest:

*Take a look at the survey responses at the beginning of this section. How many of those work minefields do you encounter?*
*Have you ever before considered that the source of workplace drama may be sin?*
*If sin is the source of workplace drama, are you guilty?*

# The Big "I" of Workplace Drama

If the drama is bad enough in your workplace, it erodes your desire to go to work or may cause you to leave an otherwise good job. It causes decreased productivity, HR nightmares, and a toxic work environment.

Why is that? Why do we have to contend with such a petty thing as drama in the workplace? We just looked at the root cause; now we'll look at another reason for the drama. The big "I."

## Insecurity

We all have it, which is why we have drama. Everyone is desperately insecure on some level. Everyone. We have insecurities about our looks, our abilities, and our backgrounds. Anything is fair game when it comes to insecurity. So how does insecurity equate to workplace drama? Take a look at the progression:

### 1. Insecurity Breeds Fear

When someone is insecure about something, especially their abilities, it comes out in the workplace as fear. If I am insecure about one of my abilities, and I see someone else who excels at it, it makes me insecure and fearful.

We fear because we are afraid someone will notice that we're not very good at the things we are responsible for doing, overseeing, or accomplishing. We fear others will discover our deficit in these areas and expose us. Then we might get fired, reprimanded, or discounted.

Instead of facing our fears and insecurities, we mask them under self-protection.

### 2. Fear Breeds Self-Protection

When we get afraid, our first instinct is to protect ourselves. It's the way God wired us. If we feel attacked (real or perceived), we will protect ourselves from the attacker (real or perceived). If you were fearful that someone was out to hurt you in some way, you would do whatever it takes to protect yourself.

Self-protection can be a good thing. It can protect us from danger and harm. But when self-protection takes root in our own insecurity, nothing good comes from it. Self-protection can distort our judgment. Makes sense, right?

We think we're only trying to protect ourselves. But in the end, our actions don't always warrant our response. Our response is often too extreme and in enters the drama.

### 3. Self-Protection Breeds Drama

If you are going out of your way to protect yourself, your reputation, or your job, you have probably fallen into . . . *The Drama Zone* (cue the background music's scary crescendo).

We enter The Drama Zone when we attempt to justify our actions and our tendency to lash out on those around us. When we lash out, we are in our self-protective mode, which is just fear that came out of our own insecurities. Does any of this sound familiar?

I recently had lunch with a young woman who was experiencing The Drama Zone in her workplace. After she told me the entire story, I looked at her and said (about the co-worker causing the drama), "She's just scared and trying to protect herself. That's why she did what she did."

"I never thought of it that way, but it's true," was her reply.

You see, I don't think anyone sets out to be the Drama Queen or King in your workplace. They get off course with their insecurities, fear, and self-protection. And next thing you know, they're there in The Drama Zone, just trying to get out unscathed. They aren't sure how to get out, and you get caught in the crossfire.

This is where we, as believers, enter in. God has called us to be peacemakers. To build others up, instead of tearing them down. To speak God's grace and love into the lives of others.

Workplace drama is an opportunity for women of faith to shine their lights. We know we are secure in God's love and grace, but your co-worker doesn't. An unbeliever has little security apart from their own self-protection (and we all know what that leads to, right?).

Think about the big "I" of workplace drama. Think about the insecurity, fear, and self-protection that your co-workers exhibit when they enter The Drama Zone. Pray for God to give you the words that will help them feel more secure.

"Gracious words are like a honeycomb, sweetness to the soul and health to the body" (Prov. 16:24 [English Standard Version]).

Words are powerful things. Think of the enormous impact of our words. According to a study by Dr. LouAnn Brizendine,[11] the average woman speaks twenty thousand words per day. Of the many words we speak, how many of them help the listener? The right words can build a person up and diffuse a tense situation.

### *Your words could be the catalyst for changing your co-worker's life.*

Your words could be the other big "I": Inspiration.

★ ★ **Let's be honest:** ★ ★

*What are your workplace insecurities?*
*Do you fear someone will find out about your lack of abilities?*
*Do you ever go into self-protection mode?*
*How intentional are you in your words?*

## Workplace Drama: How David Dealt with It

You get to work and what do you see? The Bully of the workplace. Like a formidable giant waiting for you to cross the threshold so they can knock you and/or others to the ground. Maybe there is a whole group of them facing you.

The truth is, you were thinking of them on the way to work. You were imagining what new ploy they might hatch today. What is today's scheme for pushing their way into the boss's good graces? Who will they pick on today?

Or perhaps it's the critic, the one who finds fault with everything anyone does. They spend most of their time complaining about management's new decision or degrading their co-workers.

Maybe there's a person in your workplace who is angry all the time, or always jealous of others with malicious intent.

No matter the type of person creating your personal workplace drama, you can deal with their negative presence. Rest easy. You are not alone.

Even David, the future King of Israel, dealt with workplace drama.

You remember David from the Bible: the shepherd boy who became king, called by God Himself as "a man after God's own heart."

David wasn't perfect by any means, but he seemed to know how to handle those who opposed him. Let's look at how David handled workplace drama:

## THE BULLY:

Goliath, the Bully, was a big, tall drink of water who worked for the Philistines (1 Sam. 17). He came out and taunted the Israelite army every day, twice a day, for forty days. Everyone was afraid of Goliath, and rightly so. But David wasn't afraid.

David understood who had his back. He understood that it was God's battle, not his. And he understood that sometimes you have to stand and fight.

Too many Christians these days think that meek means weak. Nothing could be further from the truth. Meekness is strength under control. It means you are strong, but you know how to control your strength.

As much as we dislike confrontation, sometimes it's the only solution. But be sure to practice confrontation like David did, with God's power and not your own.

## THE CRITIC:

Not only does David deal with a Bully, he also faces the Critic, Eliab. Eliab was David's own brother who assigned false motives to David. He criticized David for doing the right thing.

You will face that, as a woman of faith in the workplace. You will choose to do what is right and it will cause others to criticize you for it. They may call you a "goody two-shoes" all day long, but you choose to do what is right anyway, and let God handle the rest.

That's what David did when Eliab criticized him. He knew Eliab was wrong, but he didn't focus on Eliab's faults. Instead, he kept pursuing the right path, regardless of Eliab's criticisms.

## THE JEALOUS:

After David defeats the giant Goliath, he is immediately given a job working for the King. King Saul. But Saul becomes jealous of David's popularity and abilities. Most of all, he becomes jealous of God's presence with David (1 Sam. 18).

When you face the Jealous in your workplace, try to understand what they are jealous about. It probably has less to do with what you have accomplished in the workplace, and more to do with the peace and joy you have as a result of your relationship with God. Although, I doubt anyone in your workplace will attempt to pin you to the wall with a spear like Saul tried to do to David!

What did David do in this situation? He took the path of wise retreat. He knew when he needed to make himself scarce. Sometimes it is a good thing to walk away from a situation.

## THE ANGRY:

Fast forward several years and David—along with his men, wives, and children—is on the run from Saul (1 Sam. 30). One day, while the men are on a raid, the Amalekites come and destroy David's camp and take all the women and children hostage. When the men return and find out what has happened, they cry their eyes out and then they talk of killing David. His own men want to stone him to death! Have you ever faced such hostility in the workplace? I doubt it. What does David do? He found strength in the Lord (1 Sam. 30:6). David didn't try to reason with the ones who wanted to kill him. Instead he sought out the Lord, and the Lord told him how to fix the problem.

Working with these types of people is rough, no question. You may be saying, "But you don't know the kind of drama I have to face." You're right, I don't. But God does. He knows the details of every workplace drama situation you are facing. And He also knows how to solve them.

God gives us His Word and tells us stories, like the ones involving David, to help us. He helps us figure out HOW to live in this world, how to interact with those around us. He helps us deal with the Bully, the Critic, the Jealous, and the Angry.

God allows difficult people—sandpaper people who rub you the wrong way—into your life to be faith-stretchers. Their existence helps you grow in your dependence on God and gives you opportunities to live for God and trust Him for the results.

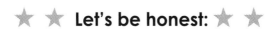

### ★ ★ Let's be honest: ★ ★

*Which workplace drama type are you dealing with in your workplace?*
*Which of David's tips can you use to help you deal with them?*
*Do you have any sandpaper people at your workplace? If so, how is God using them to stretch your faith and grow your love?*

## Seven Ways to Handle the Drama

If you didn't see the type of drama you face in your workplace above, here's a quick reference for handling any drama in a way that honors God.

### 1. Seek Peace:

"If it is possible, as far as it depends on you, live at peace with everyone" (Rom. 12:18 [New International Version]).

When dealing with workplace drama, the first tool is to seek peace. Notice God says here, "as much as depends on you." You can't control what others do, but you can control what you do to others.

**Seek to live in peace with those around you in your workplace calling.**

Sometimes, that will mean that you walk away from a conversation. Sometimes, you will bite your tongue while someone talks. Sometimes, you will need to pray for ways to seek peace. If you seek to live at peace, in God's power, He will honor your desire and give you ways to accomplish His will.

## 2. Keep Secrets:

"A gossip goes around telling secrets, but those who are trustworthy can keep a confidence" (Prov. 11:13 [New Living Translation]).

Keeping secrets is important when dealing with workplace drama. It stops the flow of gossip and builds confidence between you and others in your workplace. If they can trust you with their secrets, they can trust you to share the deeper truths of God and the hope that He provides. Go ahead and tell the Lord what you heard, but don't tell anyone else.

## 3. Be Nice:

"Don't let evil conquer you, but conquer evil by doing good" (Rom. 12:21 [New Living Translation]).

Being nice goes a long way. When you are nice to others in your workplace (even when they are not), you are doing things God's way.

When you face the Bully, the Critic, the one who wants to sabotage your career, remember this verse and remember that God will bless your obedience to it.

God's goodness triumphs over mankind's evil every time. You may not see immediate results, but no one can resist genuine kindness. And people like the Bully, the Critic, and the Saboteur may not have a lot of people who treat them with kindness. Think of the impact you could have on them!

## 4. Be Honest:

"Instead, we will speak the truth in love, growing in every way more and more like Christ, who is the head of his body, the church" (Eph. 4:15 [New Living Translation]).

This can be a difficult one and will require the Holy Spirit to guide you, but speaking the truth is a powerful thing when it's done in love. When your heart attempts to give the love of God to a co-worker, your words of truth will bring healing.

Some people are never faced with the truth of their behavior, their lies, their effect on others, or even the effect that their behavior has on themselves. Speaking truth can be a transformative way to handle the drama, if done tactfully and with love. Just remember to focus on the problem and not the person.

## 5. Be the Example:

"And you yourself must be an example to them by doing good works of every kind. Let everything you do reflect the integrity and seriousness of your teaching" (Titus 2:7 [New Living Translation]).

If you aren't walking the walk, you have no business talking the talk. This is not a holier-than-thou attitude; it's about being an authentic believer and reflecting what you teach. Once others know you are a believer, they will watch you. They will wait to see if you are the real deal or just another church-going hypocrite. This is not about being perfect, but owning your mistakes and lifting up the grace of God in your life.

## 6. Pray for Them:

"But I say, love your enemies! Pray for those who persecute you!" (Mt. 5:44 [New Living Translation]).

These words are straight from the heart of God. You cannot pray for someone and be mad at them at the same time.

**The most difficult, drama-inducing person in your workplace should be at the top of your prayer list.**

Let's be real, you spend more waking hours with that difficult person than you do with your own family. So pray for them.

No one is a lost cause. No one is beyond hope as long as they are alive and breathing. If God did a miracle in your heart, He can do a miracle in the heart of your co-worker who hails down a drama storm in your workplace. Nothing is too hard for God. Pray, and keep on praying.

**7. Look in the Mirror:**

"Why do you look at the speck of sawdust in your brother's eye and pay no attention to the plank in your own eye? How can you say to your brother, 'Let me take the speck out of your eye,' when all the time there is a plank in your own eye? You hypocrite, first take the plank out of your own eye, and then you will see clearly to remove the speck from your brother's eye" (Mt. 7:3–5 [New International Version]).

Wow! Zinger! Straight from the mouth of Jesus. Sometimes the source of the workplace drama is . . . me. It's . . . you. It's important to take a step back and check to see if we are contributing to the drama that is present in the workplace. Let's face it, sometimes we lose sight of our purpose and let our emotions spill onto every person we encounter and every place we step foot.

Stop and do a plank check. Ask the Lord to show you areas where you are contributing to the drama in your workplace, and then ask Him to dig it out of you. Get rid of the plank in your eye so you can effectively minister to others with sawdust in theirs.

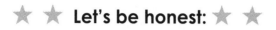

## Let's be honest:

*How hard is it to pray for someone who is making your life difficult?*
*Do you have a hard time keeping secrets?*
*Are you contributing to the drama in your workplace?*

# Workplace Discrimination

If you have been in the workforce for any length of time, you have probably experienced discrimination of some type.

Maybe you have experienced gender discrimination, due to being a woman in the workplace. Maybe you were overlooked for promotions, paid less, or treated differently because of your gender.

Perhaps you have experienced racial discrimination. The color of your skin or your ethnic background prompted others to define your abilities or potential.

Or maybe you have faced age discrimination and were overlooked for a position due to your "mature" years.

Whatever your situation, it's safe to say that we have all experienced some type of discrimination in our workplace calling.

I've been there. Although "sweetie" and "babe" aren't my given names, I've heard them.

I've had to fight to make a salary commensurate to my male counterparts.

I've had my advice passed over, only to watch a male counterpart, with the exact same advice, praised for his insight and contribution.

This topic is all over the media, but little progress is being made.

People will continue to discriminate against others due to gender, race, or age as long as human beings are in places of power. Why?

Every human has biases. You have them too, even if you don't realize it. Within our flawed human nature is a natural tendency to align ourselves with those who are like us. We give preference to them without thinking. Birds of a feather flock together.

It's not right. In fact, it's wrong and sinful and against the heart of God. God has created everybody in His image, regardless of color or gender. God created and loves even those who oppose Him and declare He doesn't exist.

So what is a woman of God in the workplace to do? How do we deal with workplace discrimination that honors God and guards our hearts from becoming cynical?

God, and God's people, are no strangers to discrimination. God's chosen people, Israel, have faced—and still face—discrimination all over the world. We may have trouble getting a promotion, but there are country leaders who are determined to destroy entire nations because of their nationality.

Scripture bears out three different options for dealing with discrimination in the workplace. Before we look at those paths, it is elemental to understand the real reasons behind discrimination.

## 1. Sin Nature:

People who have a relationship with God have biases, but people who do not have a relationship with God have even more. Why? Because they still have a sinful nature. You, as a believer, have a new nature in Christ. Others are not so fortunate. They have not yet experienced the beauty of God's grace, which allows us to see our own faults and the faults of others in the light of God's mercy.

Do not expect an unbeliever to act like a believer. It's impossible. They are powerless to say no to sin and their sinful nature. So it's no surprise then when they treat you differently based on your gender, race, or age. I'm not excusing the behavior, just explaining it.

## 2. Spiritual Warfare:

You only have one enemy in this world, and it isn't the person who discriminates against you. It's satan. Satan hates you. He wants nothing more than to see you discouraged, distracted, and disengaged from your relationship with God. If satan can get your eyes off of God and onto others, or yourself, he wins. And he knows it. Satan wants to destroy you and he will do anything to bring about that destruction, including using discrimination. Satan also loves to divide before conquering. Can you think of anything more divisive than discrimination?

If we can see the discrimination we face through the eyes of God— if we can view the people involved with God's heart—we will go a long way toward resolving discrimination in the workplace.

## 3. Self-View:

One premise that is necessary prior to exploring how to deal with discrimination in the workplace is to understand who you are in Christ.

You are a daughter of the Almighty King. Beloved and cherished. You are an amazing creation formed by the hand of the same God that made the universe in all its splendor. You are unique, created for purposes that God had in mind for you before you were born.

You are not a Wonder Woman label. You cannot be lumped together into a category of gender, race, or age. You belong to something better than this world. You were not created to fit into the molds of this world, but rather to conform to the beautiful image of the Son, who God the Father loves, just as He loves you.

The sooner you realize who you are in Christ, the easier it will be to not allow this world's definitions to define you.

### Be who God made you to be—no more, no less.

The choice is yours. Will you start the process by seeking God and seeing yourself as God sees you? Or will you decide to take the labels of Wonder Woman to heart and view the situation through your own eyes?

With that mindset in place, let's look at three God-centered ways to handle the issue of discrimination in the workplace. Remember, we receive various Actual Wonder Woman lies and labels from the world, media, friends, and family. Yet, our ultimate source for truth and information needs to come from God.

### If we filter everything through the lens of God's Word, we will never make the wrong decision.

But before we continue, I need to lay out a big, fat disclaimer: if you feel threatened or harassed in your workplace, you need to use the tools available to you through your HR department. They have those tools in place for a reason, so use them.

Here are the steps to deal with discrimination in the workplace:

### 1. Tell God First

God alone knows all the facts and circumstances regarding the treatment you are receiving.

Before they invaded Israel, the Assyrians began to taunt the people and sent King Hezekiah a letter with all kinds of threats and warnings. Before he did anything, King Hezekiah went into the Lord's presence and laid the letter out in front of Him. God didn't need to read the letter (God knew the words in the letter already), but Hezekiah's act showed his dependence and trust in his all-powerful God to handle the situation (2 Kings 19).

The same is true for us. When faced with discrimination in the workplace, it is no surprise to God. He saw it coming from a mile away.

The first step is to spend time alone with God and talk to Him about it. Before you talk to a co-worker, friend, spouse, or lawyer, talk to God. "God, did you see what they just did/said?"

The act of going to God with the issue first shows you acknowledge Him to be in control of ALL things, including the act of discrimination perpetrated against you.

## 2. Seek God's Wisdom

When discrimination takes place, emotions are often sent into a whirlwind. When I've experienced discrimination, I have felt anger, disbelief, rage, embarrassment, and shock. And that was just in the first minute! I have learned the hard way to pause when emotions run high. When I am in a heightened emotional state of mind, my ability to think logically diminishes and my decision-making skills leave the building.

After telling God, it's time to seek God's wisdom.

Have you ever met a wise person? They are calm and almost emotionless. They listen more than they talk. They give out small but profound bits of advice that are almost always right on the mark.

God is the wisest ever. God is the source of wisdom.

*God never gives the wrong advice,
and He's always willing to give it.*

God tells us about asking for wisdom in the book of James:

"If you need wisdom, ask our generous God, and he will give it to you. He will not rebuke you for asking" (Jas. 1:5 [New Living Translation]).

If you ask for wisdom, God will give it to you. God is not hiding His wisdom behind His back, or holding it just out of your reach. He wants you to be wise.

When we ask for wisdom from God, we are acknowledging we don't know what we are doing and He does. It is worshipful to ask God what to do in a situation; He is the only One who knows the right answer.

## 3. Do God's Will

Now that you have told God about the discrimination you face and sought His wisdom on the matter, you are ready to act. How God leads you will determine which path you take.

Will God lead you to do nothing? Maybe. Perhaps God will lead you to be silent in the matter. To take the wrong silently, as Jesus did.

Will God lead you to fight? Maybe. He may lead you to name the injustice and expose the wrong.

Which is the best way to go? That depends. It depends on your situation, God's plan for your life, and how He plans to use the discrimination you faced for His purposes and His glory.

One thing you can be certain of: you must do God's will in the matter. God always blesses obedience. If He leads you to do nothing, make sure you do nothing. If He leads you to fight, make sure you fight.

On the surface, these may seem to be trite "Christian-ease" ways of dealing with pervasive problems. But in reality, these are the steps we should take in every situation we deal with in the workplace.

Notice that God is at the center of each step. With God as your perfect guide and loving Father, you can face anything this life, and your work, throws at you.

# Doing Right is Never Wrong

Integrity: honesty, uprightness, moral character.

It's a noble sounding word. It conjures visions of knights in armor, seated on muscular stallions. Stalwart and invincible. Perhaps you see a minister or pastor, one who is unwavering in their moral and ethical beliefs.

Do you ever picture yourself? Would you define yourself as a woman of integrity? Would you like to?

Integrity is not some unattainable virtue relegated only to those who have been to seminary; it is a quality available to all of us.

> *Integrity is not a pill you take or a book you read.*
> *Integrity is a choice.*

Actually, it's a lot of choices.

Integrity is about acting in line with your beliefs. It's not following a list of dos and don'ts. It's choosing the right way, God's way, every time. Easier said than done? Not when you break it down into those million and one choices. Let me show you:

- You have a 9:00 meeting. You show up prepared.

- Your boss asks if you finished working on your assigned report. You tell them not yet, instead of saying, "Yes," when it isn't finished.

- No one will know if you come back late from lunch. You come back on time.

It's the little things, the things we do when no one is watching. It's being true to our beliefs, instead of caving into the pressure. It's placing our values above our own personal gain.

### Integrity is the opposite of hypocrisy.

It's not about perfection, it's about progress. God doesn't expect us to be perfect; neither does anyone else. But those around us are watching to see if we are going to live out our beliefs.

For example, I once had a boss who told me that if a certain person called, I was to say that he was out of the office. Because God values honesty, I value honesty.

I answered his request by saying, "The only way I can say you are out of the office is if you are out of the office. If I can lie for you, then I can lie to you, and I don't think you want me lying to you."

Guess what? He didn't fire me. He didn't reprimand me. He said I had a good point, and never asked me to lie for him again.

Integrity always wins. Even if he did fire me for that, I would leave with my head held high, knowing that I was true to my beliefs and my desire to please God above all else.

Little "right" daily choices train us for the big "right" choices that will come someday. Opportunities to practice integrity abound in today's workplace culture.

It isn't a matter of "if," but "when." You will face the choice to do the right thing or the wrong thing. To choose God's way or man's way. What will you do? Will you take on the challenge of integrity training? Will you commit in your heart to do the right thing?

How do you know the right thing? Isn't it relative? Doesn't it depend on the situation?

**Integrity never depends on the situation, but always depends on character.**

God is the only source for knowing the right action. God's way is always right. God's way never changes. God's way doesn't depend on the situation. God's way is only found by reading God's Word. If you want to know how to deal with a matter of integrity training, go to God's Word.

God's Word has an answer for every situation you face, every ethical dilemma, and every workplace struggle. Finding God's way in His Word is also a choice.

- It's a choice to get up fifteen minutes earlier and feed yourself from the Word of Life.

- It's a choice to post verses where you can see them throughout the week to remind you of His ways and His promises.

- It's a choice to ask God for wisdom and follow through by obeying His commands.

I never said any of these choices would be easy. They aren't easy. But if you want to be a woman of integrity who can make a stand when asked to do something wrong, you'll need to make that choice.

Whether that "wrong" is something illegal or something against your beliefs, it's still wrong. Has someone asked you to do something wrong? Maybe a supervisor asked you to lie for them. Maybe your boss told you to misplace a bill or change pricing on an invoice. Maybe a fellow employee asked you to cover for them while they took a long lunch.

According to my survey, over 23 percent of the women we spoke with have faced this situation in their workplace calling. That number likely jumps even higher when we consider the women in the survey who were asked to do something illegal. This issue of compromising your integrity is the second highest issue encountered by women of faith in the workplace, second only to workplace drama.

That means you are not alone. Others have faced the same issues. They get asked to compromise.

Sooner or later, someone will ask you to do something that goes against your beliefs. You have a choice. What you choose will form your character, shape your future, and determine your integrity. Integrity is made up of a million little choices. Making the choice to stick to your values will always be better than protecting your job.

Yes, it is scary to face those situations. I understand you're scared and uncertain. You are afraid you are going to lose your job if you say no.

You might lose your job or you might not. The one certain thing is that you will know you made the right decision when you say no to illegal activities or to things that go against your beliefs. God will bless your obedience in doing the right thing.

You are the only one who has to live with yourself; no one at work has to do that. Sometimes you will make the right choice, sometimes you won't. But God's grace is bigger than your mistakes.

I can give you a million examples of when I have made the wrong choice and compromised my values to keep the peace or save my job. But I can also give a few examples of doing the right thing.

Which is better? To do the right thing and suffer for it? Or to do the wrong thing because it is the easier path?

***By standing up to do what is right, you set the stage for future victories.***

Daniel was a man of God with uncompromising integrity from the time of his youth. He declined to eat the King's food and refused to worship or pray to the idol of the leader. Each step of the way, Daniel determined in his heart to do the right thing.

Do you know where his integrity landed him? In a den full of lions. I doubt any of us will ever end up in a den full of hungry lions because we chose to say no to our boss!

God spared Daniel's life as a blessing of his obedience. Daniel still had to spend the night in the lion's den, but he survived and became a living testimony to the ruler of the largest civilization in the known world at the time. God later called Daniel greatly beloved of God (Dan. 10:11 and 19).

God gave Daniel the power to say no to the King and yes to God. But the choice was still Daniel's.

Are you ready to make the right choice when asked to do something illegal or against your beliefs? Your integrity depends upon it.

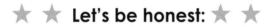

## ⭐ ⭐ Let's be honest: ⭐ ⭐

*How many times have you been asked to do something wrong?*
*How did you handle it?*
*How will you handle it in the future?*
*Will you commit to being a woman of integrity?*

# Fighting Temptation at Work

Whatever the mine you are defusing, know that you will always face the temptation to take the path of least resistance. You will always have a choice to first do what is easiest, whether that temptation involves covering up your mistakes, doing something wrong, or even flirting with a co-worker. Taking the easy way out will lead you down the path from temptation toward sin, and you'll be standing at a crucial line.

A line you never thought you'd face.

A line you said you'd never cross.

It's a standard. A value. A non-negotiable.

Yet here you are, facing the choice to do wrong.

You have allowed yourself into a situation. You were lured here, captivated by the shiny possibility of easy, and now you need to make a choice: take the bait or swim away.

What do you do when faced with temptation in your workplace calling? Are you strong enough to say, "NO!" and walk away? Temptations are a part of life; it's what you do with them that matters. Here are four practical ways to fight temptations and claim victory:

### 1. Know the source

First, take a look at the source of temptation. Where is this temptation coming from? From the person who is asking you to cross that line? No. Is God the source of your temptation? No. You are.

Look at what God has to say about the source in James:

"And remember, when you are being tempted, do not say, 'God is tempting me.' God is never tempted to do wrong, and he never tempts anyone else. Temptation comes from our own desires, which entice us and drag us away. These desires give birth to sinful actions. And when sin is allowed to grow, it gives birth to death" (Jas. 1:13–15 [New Living Translation]).

*God isn't trying to trip you up by putting temptations in your path. God is for you, not against you.*

Temptations come from your own "lower nature," or flesh. It is part of the curse of sin. Our old self follows us around like a shadow, clinging to old ways and longing for momentary pleasure and ease.

## 2. Know yourself

If the source of temptation to sin comes from within, then it makes sense to know yourself.

What environmental factors trip you up? Do certain places and people cause you to let down your guard? What inward insecurities feed your desires?

What pride in your own goodness and strength has laid a trap for you to be blind-sided by your own weaknesses? Remember what God says through Paul:

"So, if you think you are standing firm, be careful that you don't fall!" (1 Cor. 10:12 [New International Version]).

Be aware of places in your heart where you think you are standing firm. Unwrap your places of both weakness and pride and hand them over to God to take care of.

Physical conditions can also make you vulnerable to temptations. When you're tired, weak, hungry, or emotional, you will be less likely to have the presence of mind to say no. When I am having an exhausting day or feel run down, I make a deal with myself that I will make no major decisions that day. I had to learn that about myself.

Recognizing your vulnerabilities helps you fight the temptation you face.

### 3. Know your enemy

"The devil made me do it" is a phrase that gets tossed around. Let's be real: the devil doesn't make us do anything we don't already want to do (see point number one). Yes, satan has set up a world system that plays into our sinful and weak desires. He (and his cohorts) are dangling shiny lures in front of us daily. You only have to browse through the internet to see proof of that.

When you know your enemy, you can know how to ignore the bait. Satan wants nothing more than to destroy you completely. He doesn't just want to give you a bad day; he wants to take you out. He wants you to blow it, big time.

"Stay alert! Watch out for your great enemy, the devil. He prowls around like a roaring lion, looking for someone to devour" (1 Pet. 5:8 [New Living Translation]).

Remember, satan doesn't play nice and he doesn't play fair. Lions go after the weak, the sick, and those separated from the herd. They prefer easy prey. So follow the advice in Ephesians 6 to be strong and healthy and connected in the Lord.

### 4. Know your Savior

Don't try to fight temptation on your own. God never intended us to do battle without Him. God doesn't remove temptation when it comes our way; He gives us the power to endure it and always provides a way out of it.

"The temptations in your life are no different from what others experience. And God is faithful. He will not allow the temptation to be more than you can stand. When you are tempted, he will show you a way out so that you can endure" (1 Cor. 10:13 [New Living Translation]).

God is ready and more than willing to help us when we face temptation, but we need to ask for the help. When you are standing there at that line, the one you said you would never cross, ask God to show you the way out. The way out is there, God promises us that.

• Ask for it.

• Look for it.

• Take it.

Know that God is for you, not against you. He loves you more than you will ever know.

Will you be successful at fighting temptation every time? You have tools for victory; it's just a matter of using them. But if you do give in to temptation, know that God is gracious, slow to anger, and plenteous in mercy.

You will make mistakes along the way. You will do things in your workplace you wish you hadn't. Don't be discouraged. Realize that your God is a God of second, third, and umpteenth chances. Own your mistakes, even to your co-workers. By owning your mistakes, you show clear evidence that you are set apart, different.

> **People who don't know Christ attempt to cover, hide, and pin their mistakes on others. You are called to be different.**

• Openly admit them.

• Ask for forgiveness from God and others.

•Do whatever you can to correct the mistakes.

•Learn from the mistakes.

•Ask God to help you resist making the same mistakes.

Then get up and keep going. *That* is how you will win at work.

  **Let's be honest:**

*How many times have you found yourself standing
at the line of temptation?
What got you there? Your weaknesses? Your pride? Your fatigue?
Where does satan tug at you the most?
Do you look for the way out when you are tempted? Or do you look for
how you can get away with it?*

# PART FOUR

# SOAR
# IN FAITH

*With hollow bones a bird learns how to fly*
*Not once despising frame all delicate,*
*But pushed without the nest her wings to try,*
*Fast finds the air till flight's inveterate –*
*And pauses not to ponder nor to care*
*How fragile are her limbs amidst her flight,*
*But boldly lifts her wings against the air*
*And mounts the wind all ignorant of fright.*
*And so each day, until she dies, she lives.*
*She soars aloft, aloud, and all replete,*
*Content with gifts that her Creator gives,*
*Her weakness making all her life complete.*
*Who curses frailty wisdom needs implore,*
*For only those whose bones are hollow soar. —Anon*

You are made to soar. Just as the eaglet in our earlier story belonged in the sky and not the barnyard, God made you to soar in your faith.

Soar in a growing faith relationship with your loving, Heavenly Father.

Soar in work, relationships, and daily life.

Soar, in spite of weakness and frailty.

Soar, in spite of trials and troubles.

Soar to heights previously unexplored.

How do you soar like that? By developing a faith that soars, continues soaring higher, and goes on soaring to the end.

CHAPTER TEN

# FAITH THAT SOARS

Faith that soars is a faith with perspective. The perspective of life's brevity. The perspective that focuses on the end game. The perspective that knows boldness is required, because life is short. The perspective that faith is a daily, life-long journey, not a sprint to the finish. The perspective that faithfulness and foundational truths are more valuable than fleeting accomplishments. The perspective that rest and trust are more important than action.

> *But those who trust in the Lord will find new strength.*
> *They will soar high on wings like eagles.*
> *They will run and not grow weary.*
> *They will walk and not faint.*

(Isa. 40:31 [New Living Translation])

## Faith That Soars Is Bold

If you knew you only had a few more years to walk this earth, would it change the way you live? Let's say you still had to go to work every week, your family was the same, and you were not independently wealthy.

- Would you behave with integrity and honesty, instead of hiding behind shortcuts and compromise?

- Would you have boldness in sharing the life-saving truth of the Gospel with others, instead of being afraid of what someone thinks of you?

- Would you give words of love and encouragement to those around you, instead of being critical and angry?

- Would you spend your resources of time, love, and money differently, instead of thinking of your own wants and needs?

- Would you step out in faith, instead of letting your fears and insecurities stand in the way of your God-given dreams?

What would change in your life if you knew your time here was limited? Because it is. A few fleeting years is all we're given before we pass into eternity.

"You have made my life no longer than the width of my hand. My entire lifetime is just a moment to you; at best, each of us is but a breath" (Ps. 39:5 [New Living Translation]).

To God, our life here on earth is but a moment, a breath. Think of how many breaths you take in a minute. A breath is short and over quickly. Some days it seems like we have time to do all the things we know God is calling us to. Other days, we wish for more hours in the day.

Time is a relative thing, but we are all given the same amount of it. Time is the great equalizer; we are all given 24/7/365 for as many years as we have here on earth.

We forget that it will end someday. Life will be over and it will seem brief when we stand before eternity. Then, we will understand that the above verse is all too true.

As women of faith, we know that it matters what we send ahead into eternity. We know that we should treasure things above, that we should make the most of our time here on earth. We believe that our investment in other people will last beyond our deaths.

But how do we live that out?

How do we act on what we know by faith in our hearts? Two words: Be bold.

That's it. Be bold. As women, we often take the non-confrontational, passive approach to life. It isn't because we are weak. It isn't because we are not capable. It's because we are not bold.

• We shrink back when God tells us to stand.

• We shut our mouths when God tells us to speak out.

• We hold back when God tells us to go forward.

It's time to say, "ENOUGH!" It's time to be bold.

We serve the One and Only, All-Powerful, Almighty, Creator, Father, God. No one and nothing is more powerful than God. And He is your God. He is your Friend. He is your biggest Cheerleader. God is rooting for you. God is ready to empower you to be bold.

*"For the Kingdom of God is not just a lot of talk; it is living by God's power" (1 Cor. 4:20 [New Living Translation]).*

*"Remember the Lord your God. He is the one who gives you power to be successful, in order to fulfill the covenant he confirmed to your ancestors with an oath"*

(Deut. 8:18 [New Living Translation]).

*"I also pray that you will understand the incredible greatness of God's power for us who believe him. This is the same mighty power that raised Christ from the dead and seated him in the place of honor at God's right hand in the heavenly realms"*

(Eph 1:19–20 [New Living Translation]).

God's power empowers His believers to be bold in living out our faith. The same power that parted seas and made the blind see is available to you and me. You and I don't have the power to be bold in our lives, but we do have bold power available for us to use.

These truths should not mire us in the guilt of wishing we had done more. They are a call to arms, a cry of promised victory, a shout to be bold from here on out because faith that soars is bold.

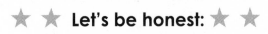

### Let's be honest:

*Do you want faith that soars?*
*Are you living like your life is brief?*
*Are you as bold as you want to be?*
*Will you tap into the power God makes available to you?*

## Faith That Soars Is Centered, Not Balanced

You remember the teeter-totter, right? It was impossible to keep balanced, and someone always ended up with a sore rear-end. Did you ever try to balance one of those by standing in the middle? Even in the middle, it never stayed balanced. And if you did manage to balance that awkward hunk of wood and metal, it only lasted for a nanosecond.

Wonder Woman comes creeping in with her lies and says we need work-life balance, which means one side or the other will go down.

If we put our effort into the lives God has called us to, our work will suffer.

If we put effort into our work God has called us to do, our lives will suffer.

Are we supposed to perch between the middle of the two, attempting to dole out our effort in perfect proportion to keep everything in perfect balance?

IMPOSSIBLE!

Is that supposed to be something we are striving toward? Something that is short-lived and impossible to achieve?

Faith that soars shows a better way: a God-centered life.

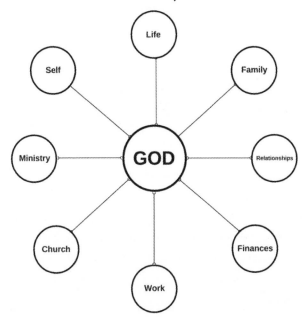

Think *wheel* instead of *teeter-totter*. God is the hub. Our relationship with God is the center; it is the balance. Every other area of our lives springs out from Him, because they are all gifts that He has given us. They all come from Him.

When our relationship with God is at the center of our lives, everything will receive the appropriate time, resources, and effort. We will have balance in all areas of our lives, guaranteed.

It's just that simple. Simple, not *easy*. But it's not impossible either (like balancing on a teeter-totter is).

*If we focus on building and growing our relationship with God, everything else will be a manifestation of that relationship.*

The wheel of life will turn in smooth progression. We will see progress and forward movement in every area of our lives. And we will be centered. We will have peace and calm in the midst of all the areas of our lives that are vying for our attention and presence.

If we get away from that God-focus and start to focus more on anything on the outer edge of the wheel, life will be a wobbly mess. To fix the wobbly mess, we will jump to the next thing on the wheel to try to stabilize that, and the next, and so on, and so on. But when we stop the crazy spinning, jumping, and wobbling and get back to the center, balance will return.

Come to the wheel. Experience the true balance and peace that only God can give. God has been waiting for you for a long time. He watches you struggle and longs to release you from yourself, your independence, your self-will. Surrender your life to Him and watch Him do amazing things!

##  Let's be honest:

*Are you still trying to find a work-life balance
that is impossible to achieve?
Are you on the wheel, knowing God is important, but hanging out on
the edges, wobbling, and trying to balance a moving wheel in a way that
defies physics? Come back to the center.
Having experienced the peace of God, do you think you no longer need
Him? Do you think He has left you to go it alone? He has promised to
never leave nor forsake you. Come back to Him. He is waiting for His
beloved daughter with open arms.*

Get God-centered this week and you will find balance, peace, and faith that soars.

## Faith That Soars Is F.A.T.

What if I told you God wants you to be F.A.T.? That being F.A.T. is key to faith that soars?

Whew! Finally! I can have a reason for my tummy pooch, my muffin top, and my cellulite. Yippee!

Well, not so fast. God does want us to take care of the body He has given us, but that isn't His priority. Yes, God doesn't look at the outside; He looks at the heart.

> *Internal value always takes precedence over external appearances.*

In 1 Samuel 16:7 God talks to Samuel about who will be the next King of Israel. Samuel thinks it should be Eliab. In fact, scripture says he took one look at Eliab and thought he should be king.

"But the LORD said to Samuel, 'Don't judge by his appearance or height, for I have rejected him. The LORD doesn't see things the way you see them. People judge by outward appearance, but the LORD looks at the heart'" (1 Sam. 16:7 [New Living Translation]).

God had other plans. God had other priorities. God wasn't scoping the land for the best-looking, most gifted person to lead His treasured possession, Israel. God was looking for someone who was F.A.T. and He found that person in David. God called David "a man after God's own heart" before David was anointed King (1 Sam. 13:14).

The scripture is full of stories of the people God chose because they were F.A.T. Ruth, Joseph, Esther, Mary, Peter, and Paul are all examples. What was it about these people that made them stand out? Why did God choose them over others? They were F.A.T.:

•Faithful

•Available

•Teachable

That's it. Three simple things that mean the world to God. Become F.A.T. and you'll become a woman after God's own heart.

## FAITHFUL

This is the idea of being loyal and steadfast. Why is this important to God? Because He is faithful.

"God will make this happen, for he who calls you is faithful" (1 Thess. 5:24 [New Living Translation]).

"Understand, therefore, that the LORD your God is indeed God. He is the faithful God who keeps his covenant for a thousand generations and lavishes his unfailing love on those who love him and obey his commands" (Deut. 7:9 [New Living Translation]).

It's one of His many attributes. God is steadfast and loyal; He keeps His promises to us. He always follows through on His word. He can be counted on. As we experience God's faithfulness in our lives, we gain a desire to be faithful in return. As we grow in grace and knowledge of Jesus, we begin to look like Him. The closer we get to God, the more faithful we become.

•Are you faithful?

•Can God count on you to follow through?

•Is your loyalty to Him evident in your life?

Or are you a "come-and-go" Christian? Do you only follow God when it's easy to do so? Are you loyal to His love for you when times are tough as well as when times are good? I recently finished reading through the book of Job. If you want an example of a faithful follower, look at Job, who praised God in times of plenty and in times of disaster. He never turned His back on God.

Or what about Joseph, who endured brothers who hated him and sold him into slavery? He was wrongfully imprisoned and yet remained faithful to God.

"To the faithful you show yourself faithful; to those with integrity you show integrity" (2 Sam. 22:26 [New Living Translation]).

## AVAILABLE

This idea centers around being present and ready to use. Are you at God's disposal?

God owns us; we have been bought with a price. But we have also been given free will. We get to choose every moment of every day if we will make ourselves available for God's use. God will not force us. He is a gentleman, always asking and inviting us to come to Him.

Can God call on you like He called on Samuel, Moses, Nehemiah, and Mary? Will He hear you respond, "Here I am, Lord"? Can you set your agenda and plans and goals aside and surrender to whatever and wherever God calls you?

Why is this important to God? Because God is available. Any day or the year, any hour, you can call on God and He will be there for you. God is omnipresent. He is everywhere at once, available to whomever needs Him.

God is the great "I AM," the One. The one who is ever-present, ever-available.

Once you became God's daughter, you simultaneously became part of God's army. God, through Paul's letter to Timothy, talks about how we are like soldiers in His army. He admonishes us with these words:

"Endure suffering along with me, as a good soldier of Christ Jesus. Soldiers don't get tied up in the affairs of civilian life, for then they cannot please the officer who enlisted them" (2 Tim. 2:3–4 [New Living Translation]).

Makes sense, doesn't it? A soldier reports for duty and awaits orders. What about you?

•Are you available?

•Do you report for duty daily?

•Do you surrender each day to God?

Do you surrender your life, your plans, and your dreams into His loving hands and wait for orders? Or do you struggle to hold onto your daily plans and hope you can squeeze God in there somewhere?

## TEACHABLE

This is the idea of being eager to learn and able to be taught. Why is this important to God? Because He knows everything and we do not.

I didn't finish my bachelor's degree until about four years ago. One lesson I learned during the process was that I had much more to learn. I love to read. I am always seeking out information. I know we never stop learning.

Yet, my love for learning doesn't always make me teachable. It's a part of it—being eager to learn—but the other part is being able to be taught. I can love to learn new things, but without putting them into practice, I can't say that I am teachable.

God longs to impart His wisdom to us. He longs for us to gain knowledge about Him and His Word. I can read the Bible every day and attend Bible studies until I'm blue in the face, but if I never apply what I learn, I am not teachable.

God wants us to take what we learn from Him and put it into practice. It's called application. It's called wisdom. I can memorize verses and recite the books of the Bible in order, but if I am not living out what I learn, what good does it do me? It's more of a way to show off to others than it is to please God. Remember, He looks at the heart.

The crucial part of being teachable is admitting we don't know it all. Coming to God and asking Him to teach you is a way to humble yourself before God. Presenting yourself to the master teacher will ensure that you have a receptive heart that is teachable.

Jesus said, "Take my yoke upon you. Let me teach you, because I am humble and gentle at heart, and you will find rest for your souls" (Mt. 11:29 [New Living Translation]).

How about you? Are you teachable?

•Are you eager to learn?

•Are you able to be taught?

•Will you seek to apply what God teaches you?

•Are you willing to learn from your mistakes?

Or are you thinking you know enough to get by? Do you feel like you don't need more wisdom? Are you afraid of what God will show you about yourself and your heart when He teaches you?

We make life pretty complicated and hard sometimes. We try to give ourselves too many rules to follow, too many to-do lists, too many "have-tos." God keeps things simple for us.

•Faithful

•Available

•Teachable

Three things that can simplify your life, empower your walk with God, and give you faith that soars.

## ★ ★ Let's be honest: ★ ★

*Are you F.A.T. for God?*
*Which one of these things do you struggle with the most?*
*Will you commit in your heart to focus more on the inside*
*than on the outside?*

Dedicate yourself to being F.A.T., just the way God wants you, and your faith will soar.

# Faith That Soars Is Obedient

Everyone is searching for the secret to success. There are thousands of books and theories on how to achieve success, what success looks like, and how to be successful in succeeding.

But God's way to success is much different than any of the ways you read about in books.

God wraps up the definition of success in one word:

### Obedience

It doesn't sound glamorous or easy. It sounds hard, and sometimes it is. But it is a lot easier than you think. It's not a long list of rules and regulations; it's just taking one step of obedience at a time. God doesn't show us the whole picture and all His reasons for leading us to certain places in our lives. He just asks us to trust Him and obey.

### Each time we take a step of obedience in faith, God increases our faith.

If we choose not to obey God's requests, we will stall in our growth, feel unsatisfied and restless, and miss out on the blessings that come with obedience. Samuel said to Saul in response to his disobedience to God:

"And Samuel said, 'Has the LORD as great delight in burnt offerings and sacrifices, as in obeying the voice of the LORD? Behold, to obey is better than sacrifice, and to listen than the fat of rams'" (1 Sam. 15:22 [English Standard Version]).

Let me share with you a little of my own experience with learning that God blesses obedience.

God has led me down some unpredictable and incredible paths in life. Each path seems to require more faith than the last. Each one has tested my dependence on my Savior. Each one has required radical obedience. Each time, God blessed my obedience.

About a decade ago, God called me to start my first business. For two years, God patiently spoke through His Word and the words of others that there was a need, and I could fill it by going out on my own. I felt waves of fear, doubt, and insecurity.

- "Are you sure?" I asked.

- "Are you really sure?" I repeated, hoping for a different answer.

- "I need to know I'm hearing you right" (Or, please repeat yourself for a third time!).

And so began the four months of my "Nehemiah Experience," where I prayed and waited. I planned and prepared the business to launch, anticipating the day my King would give me the go-ahead. The day came. I lurched, then launched. It was almost like being born again, again. I was in that place where passion and purpose meet. I was in the zone that my Creator God had made just for me from before the foundation of the world.

And God blessed the obedience.

The business grew, I grew, and my faith deepened and soared to a level I had never before experienced.

Great things happen where God's faithfulness and your obedience collide.

As the years passed, I grew to be independent and relied more on my developed abilities than upon my all-powerful God. It was time to stretch again.

This time, God led me back to school to finish my bachelor's degree. Fears, doubts, and insecurities returned in full force and the questions began again:

- •"Are you sure?" I asked.

- •"Are you really sure?" I repeated, hoping for a different answer.

- •"I need to know I'm hearing you right."

I prayed and applied. Registered and bought books. I leapt from one rock of faith to another like a child crossing a creek that isn't as wide or fast-flowing as it appears. With each leap, God placed my foot on His solid ground.

And God blessed my obedience.

He enabled and empowered me to finish my degree while running a business and seeing two kids through high school. I leaned heavily upon the Lord for every paper, every exam, and every precious bit of sleep. I grew, and my faith deepened and soared higher. I came to know and trust more intimately this God that loved me, and I loved in return.

With my newfound education, it didn't take long to become more independent and self-reliant. Less faith was required, and that seemed to suit me fine. It was time to stretch again. While trail running along a river three years ago, God called me to start the non-profit organization, Working Women of Faith. Enter the same nagging doubts and fears. The same questions:

- "Are you sure?" I asked.

- "Are you really sure?" I repeated, hoping for a different answer.

- "I need to know I'm hearing you right."

I prayed, fasted, and set up Working Women of Faith the next week. I entered new territory and had much to learn. I started with baby steps and just kept moving in the direction of God's calling. I was in my element. And God blessed the obedience.

I have learned utter dependence on an all-powerful God and watched Him perform miracles through the simple act of obedience. I have met amazing people, have grown as a child of God, and have watched my faith soar.

And God blessed my obedience.

A few months ago, God called me to write this book for you. I went through all the same doubts and fears as before. But I obeyed, and the blessing of that obedience is in your hands.

 **Let's be honest:**

*Is God calling you to do something that seems impossible? We serve the God of the impossible!*
*Are you willing to obey?*
*In exchange for your obedience, God will give you faith that soars.*

# Faith That Soars
# Uses What God Gives

Do you ever feel like God is asking for more than you are capable of doing?

Are there days, months, even seasons of your life that feel like you can't take on anymore? Like you have reached your limit?

The wonderful truth is that God helps us manage all He wants us to do. God isn't expecting miracles from us; that's His job. So relax. I know it sometimes feels like everyone else is expecting miracles from you, but God isn't and that is all that matters.

So what does God expect from us?

In the parable of the talents found in Matthew 25:14–30, God reveals what He expects from us. There is a little part of a verse in this parable that you may have passed over. At the end of verse fifteen, Jesus says, "in proportion to their abilities."

Use what God gives you without comparing.

The master in this parable entrusts his servants with some of his money to oversee while he is away. He gives them the talents (resources) according, and in proportion, to their abilities. He doesn't give them more than they are capable of handling. He gives them just the right amount.

Our Master (God Almighty) knows our capabilities. He knows our abilities and gifting better than we do because He is the one who gave us these abilities.

**God will never ask us to do more than we are able to do with Him.**

Notice the "with Him" part of that statement. With God, we are capable of more than we can imagine. And apart from God, we can do nothing.

Use what God gives you without hiding or adding.

In the aforementioned parable, the servants get busy using what

God gives them. The servants who got five and ten talents went right to work, doubling what they received. The servant who only got one talent hid it. He was so afraid of messing up that he never used what the master gave him. Of all three servants, the last one was the only one rebuked and punished.

The other servants got to hear, "Well done, faithful servant!"

Why?

Because they used what God gave them, according to their abilities.

•They didn't complain.

•They didn't compare.

•They didn't hide what they were given.

God isn't asking you to do any more than those servants. He gives you opportunities according to your abilities and asks you to use them. Don't hide what God has given you out of fear of messing up. You might make mistakes along the way, but it's better to try than to hide.

Use what God gives you.

If He has given you the ability to do your job, use it.

If He has given you the opportunity to share His love with others, use it.

If He has given you a gift that can be used to bless others and bring glory to His name, use it.

The dangerous part comes when we try to extend beyond what God has given us. If the servant who was given five talents tried to take on ten, he would have failed and been discouraged and disappointed.

**Use only what God gives you
and you won't feel overwhelmed.**

Use what God gives you and you'll get more (or less).

When we choose to use what God gives us, He gives us more. When we choose to hide what He gives us, we lose what we had in the first place. Look at this verse from the end of the parable:

"To those who use well what they are given, even more will be given, and they will have an abundance. But from those who do nothing, even what little they have will be taken away" (Mt. 25:29 [New Living Translation]).

God wants to give and give in abundance and without measure because we serve a generous God. But if He can't trust you with what He has already given you, why would He give you more?

God has great things planned for your life. Things with eternal impact. But He can't do those things when we don't use what He has already given to us. Use what God gives you, and He'll give you more.

Then you too will hear the words, "Well done, good and faithful servant!"

  **Let's be honest:**

*Are you using what God has given you?*
*Have you been hiding what God gave you?*
*Is it time to say "No" to the things God isn't giving you?*
*How can you use what you have now for God's glory?*
*Using what God gives you reflects your soaring faith.*

# Faith That Soars Is Trusting

There are a few things in this physical world I fear. Spiders. Snakes. But nothing scares me more than swimming with things that are bigger than me. I fear swimming in the ocean. I had a childhood experience that leaves me terrified to swim in the ocean, lakes, and rivers to this day.

Do you know what I did on a recent vacation? I swam in the ocean. My kids are adults now, and I never swam in the ocean with them when they were little. I was too scared. But this time I thought, "What's the worst that can happen? I could get eaten by a shark and die and end up in heaven with Jesus. That sounds pretty good to me."

I decided to do a "trust fall" into God's loving arms, and I swam. It was wonderful! I can't believe I wasted all those opportunities throughout the years because I was afraid of what might happen. I had let my fear hold me back from enjoying one of God's most amazing creations. After releasing my fear, I had a truly amazing day. I savored the sensation of rising and falling with the waves, the beauty of the ocean, and the time spent on the water with my kids.

The trust fall. Falling into the arms of the everlasting God. Just fall. You don't have to understand everything. You don't have to be completely free from fear to trust.

Trust is the idea of putting all your weight onto something, like when you sit on a chair, knowing it will hold you up. You trust that it not only has the ability to hold you up, but that the ability is inherent in its makeup. God longs to give good gifts to His children. He will give you the desires of your heart.

When you trust that God can and will accomplish His plan for you, you only have to have the patience to trust in His perfect timing. God's urgency timetable isn't the same as ours because He is eternal and sees the end from the beginning.

**God's timing is perfect.
True trust comes in the waiting for His timing.**

God is trustworthy.

> *Trust in the Lord with all your heart;*
> *do not depend on your own understanding.*
> *Seek his will in all you do,*
> *and he will show you which path to take.*

(Prov. 3:5–6 [New Living Translation])

Trusting God, no matter your circumstances, no matter what decision you face, is how you have faith that soars.

  **Let's be honest:**

*How are you withholding trust from God today?*
*Are you willing to do the trust fall into God's loving arms?*
*Do you trust that God's perfect timing will be unveiled?*

# Faith That Soars Lets Go

To have faith that soars, you have to learn to let go. Let go of your will and grab hold of God's.

### Let go of your past and grab hold of God's future for you.

Let go of hurts that hold you back, and grab hold of God's healing. Too many times, we are like that last desperate leaf that clings so tightly to the frozen, barren limb. In reality, if the leaf lets go, it can fly.

God has a much better plan for your life than you do.

•Your power is limited.

•Your timing is finite.

•Your vision is short-sighted.

•Your knowledge is small.

God is all-powerful; God is eternal; God is all-seeing; God knows it all. "Let go, and let God" isn't just a cliché; it's a truth that helps your faith to soar.

There is no past that God can't heal.

There is no failure that God can't redeem.

But it requires letting go first.

"No, dear brothers and sisters, I have not achieved it, but I focus on this one thing: Forgetting the past and looking forward to what lies ahead, I press on to reach the end of the race and receive the heavenly prize for which God, through Christ Jesus, is calling us" (Phil. 3:13–14 [New Living Translation]).

God wants us to learn from our past, not cling to it.

Why do we cling to the past and risk missing the future God has for us? Because the past is comfortable. We know the past. It's familiar to us. The future is unknown, untested, and downright scary sometimes.

### Fear holds us in the past, but God is already in the future.

We can press on to reach the end of the race because, to God, the future is already here. We can press on to receive what God has in store for us with no fear, knowing He's already there.

Let go of your past so God can give you a glorious future. You must let go in order to soar.

Apply the one-hundred-year rule to your past hurts and future hopes. Ask yourself, "Will this matter in one hundred years?"

You see, in one hundred years, you'll be dead. The odds are stacked against you on that one. So ask yourself, "What will matter in a hundred years?" Your house will be a pile of rubble. Your bank account will be empty or in the hands of your descendants, who will empty it for you. That argument you had to win will be forgotten. That time you were offended or hurt by someone else won't be written down in the history books.

Let go of the things that won't matter one hundred years from now, and you will have faith that soars.

## Let's be honest:

*Are you pressing on to reach the end or looking back?*
*Are you focusing on what you did wrong or what God does right?*
*Do you spend more time regretting the past than receiving the future God has for you?*

# Faith That Soars Listens

What does God want me to do in this situation?

How will I make it through the week ahead?

Do you ever ask yourself these questions? Do you ever feel like you missed some vital step in the directions God gave you? Have you ever sensed a silence from God? I think we've all been there before.

"Whether you turn to the right or to the left, your ears will hear a voice behind you, saying, "This is the way; walk in it" (Isa. 30:21 [New International Version]).

Isn't that an amazing promise? Your ear will hear a voice behind you, like someone whispering over your shoulder, "Go right" or "Go left" or "Keep going forward."

That kind of relationship with God is what causes your faith to soar.

When Elijah ran from the threats of Jezebel and hid in a cave on Mount Horeb (1 Kings 19), he heard the voice of God. Elijah heard from God frequently (he was a prophet after all), but God wanted to make sure Elijah heard Him. So God whispered. A strong wind, earthquake, and fire all passed by Elijah, but God was not in any of them. God was in a still, small voice.

God was in the whisper. God doesn't like to shout. He loves to guide us with gentleness as our loving, heavenly Father. He longs to whisper in your ear, "This is the way; walk in it."

God promises to lead us if we turn to Him for His leadership. If we choose to go our own way, regardless of what God is saying, then we can't blame Him when we end up on the wrong path.

If you are struggling, straining to hear the voice of God for direction in your life, your workplace calling, and your family, take a moment to stop. Be silent and listen to what God is saying.

## God is always speaking, we just aren't always listening.

In order to hear God's whisper, we have to get close to Him.

- Hearing God's whisper requires spending time alone with Him daily, throughout every day. You won't hear Him if you aren't near Him. Don't rush headlong into your day without time alone with God.

- Hearing God's whisper requires being silent before Him. Sometimes we don't let God get a word in edgewise and then complain that He doesn't speak to us.

- Hearing God's whisper means following His directions. Has God whispered for you to go left and then you give Him ten reasons why "left" is a bad idea? God can't guide you if you refuse to follow His directions.

One way God speaks to us is through His Word. I firmly believe that the number one reason most believers don't have faith that soars is that they just don't read God's Word.

"BUT I DON'T HAVE TIME!" you say.

Really? The Creator of the Universe, who holds all truth and is truth, has had men write down these truths and translate them into a language you can understand. He has provided truth that can guide your life and give you comfort and answers for everything that could ever happen to you. That is the truth that you don't have time for?

Read it. Carve out fifteen minutes and just start reading the truth. It will revolutionize your life.

Fifteen minutes of truth. Because Wonder Woman is feeding you lies for eighteen hours a day, and those lies are really easy to believe. Yet, God desires to give you abundant life and faith that soars. That faith includes His truth and His whispers.

 ## Let's be honest:

*Do you feel like God is being silent right now?*
*Can you carve out some quiet time to hear Him whisper to you?*
*Are you hearing God, but not listening?*
*Commit to setting aside fifteen minutes each day to hear God speak to you through His Word.*

# Faith That Soars Rests

Rest. The word itself sounds peaceful, doesn't it?

Rest.

The word has such a beautiful ring to it.

Rest—that elusive, but ever sought after, state of ceasing from work and action.

But how does a working woman of faith rest? She's so busy!

When I think of rest, I imagine myself sitting in a chair on the beach as the waves lap my feet and the sun warms my face. Or, I think of sitting in front of a crackling fire on a cold winter's evening, reading a good book.

Those are images of rest that equate to a restful mind, a spirit at rest. An exhale from life. A pause. After all, isn't that what rest is? A pause?

These verses are all about rest. True rest. Not beaches and books. The kind of rest that requires action.

Then Jesus said, "Come to me, all of you who are weary and carry heavy burdens, and I will give you rest. Take my yoke upon you. Let me teach you, because I am humble and gentle at heart, and you will find rest for your souls" (Mt. 11:28–29 [New Living Translation]).

•Rest is not a ceasing of activity, as some may think.

•Rest is not an illusion.

•Rest is not unattainable (even for the working woman whose "work" never ends, but simply switches locations).

Rest is a promise. In the verses above, Jesus promises rest twice, but that promised rest requires action on our part. Here are the three keys to grabbing hold of the promise of rest so you can have faith that soars:

## COME

First Jesus bids us to come to Him.

### *There is no rest this world can offer that can compare to the rest found in Jesus.*

He told His disciples, and us, that the peace He gives is not like the world's peace (Jn. 14:27).

To have that long sought-after rest, we must first come to Jesus, believing that He is who He said He was: the Savior of the world. A relationship with God through Jesus is rest from the punishment and penalty of sin, rest in the knowledge of a secure home in heaven.

God's promise of rest requires that we first come to Him.

## TAKE

Second, Jesus asks us to take His yoke upon us. This is a call to partner with Jesus. A yoke harnesses the energy and power of two oxen to form one formidable team.

**_Jesus wants to partner with you in this life._**

He longs to come alongside you and walk beside you through thick and thin. That can't happen if you don't stay next to Him. He wants you yoked to Him so He can lead you step by step, side by side.

The other aspect of the yoke is submitting to the One holding the reigns. As God has directed Jesus, He is directing you as well. An ox who fights the yoke will go nowhere. The ox must submit to the yoke and the direction of the One who leads him.

## LEARN

The more I learn about the power and perfection of Jesus, the more I can rest in knowing that He holds the universe in His hands and I have nothing to fear. I don't have to work so hard to make things happen because God is making them happen on my behalf.

I would never be able to rest in those truths (and many more) if I didn't commit to daily learning from Jesus, letting Him teach me from God's Word.

**_We can't have rest apart from God._**

How often I foolishly try to go it alone! I attempt to do it all myself and then wonder why I am tired. When I come to Jesus, I admit that I am unqualified and unable to do anything apart from Him.

It is in the release of control, trusting that God can handle it, that I find rest. Rest that causes my faith to soar.

**Let's be honest:**

*Do you rest in God? Or are you trying to do everything on your own?*
*Are you partnering with Jesus in your life?*
*Are you attempting to find rest apart from God?*

# CHAPTER ELEVEN

# SOARING HIGHER

The eagle is an amazing, majestic creation of God. It's beautiful, strong, and skilled. It can see four times better than a human with 20/20 vision. It glides and soars without effort. Once, when I was running on our country road, an eagle rose from the ditch next to me and began to fly (nearly scared the spandex off me!). The power it displayed in taking flight was breathtaking!

Eagles also have the ability to know when a storm is coming. An eagle will perch high above the ground as the storm arrives, waiting for the winds to pick up. When the storm comes, the eagle uses the winds of the storm to soar until it rises above the storm.

**_The eagle does not try to escape the storm; it uses the storm to soar higher._**

What a beautiful picture of how we can and should deal with the storms of life! The storms, trials, and testing of this life are inevitable. There is no escaping pain and heartache in our lives.

Many believers, especially those who don't have faith that soars, give up when the going gets tough. To soar in faith, you'll need to figure out how to have faith that soars higher than your storms.

## Soaring Higher with Joy

Like I said before, the storms of life will come. They are inevitable. Jesus said the same thing: "I have told you these things, so that in me you may have peace. In this world you will have trouble. But take heart! I have overcome the world" (Jn. 16:33 [New International Version]).

Jesus promises that we will have trouble, trials, and hardships in this world. It's unavoidable. It will happen. In this life, you will:

•Lose a loved one.

•Have financial hardships.

•Experience failed relationships.

•Watch loved ones turn away from God.

•Lose a job.

•Grow apart from friends.

•Experience health issues.

But along with the promise of trouble, Jesus does an amazing thing. He tells us to be of good cheer.

Wait, what?! How? Why?

Because He has already overcome the world. Jesus has already overcome every trouble imaginable and, because of that, He can use those troubles in our lives to cause our faith to soar higher . . . if we let Him. Jesus promises that there is purpose in our troubles and trials.

Joseph understood this concept when He told his brothers, "You intended to harm me, but God intended it for good to accomplish what is now being done, the saving of many lives" (Gen. 50:20 [New International Version]).

Our enemy may intend to take us out and take us down through the troubles and storms of life, but God can intend those things for good to accomplish much and save many.

Over the past nine months, I have been through every trouble and storm you can think of. And yet, I can say that I am closer to God now than I was before the troubles came. I'm not overly excited to have gone through them, but I wouldn't trade them for the world! They have caused me to learn how to soar higher than the storms in my life. They have allowed me to see God in new light, increase my dependence on Him, and experience the joy that comes from Him, alone, when all else is falling apart.

This is why James was able to tell us to look at the troubles as an opportunity for great joy:

"Dear brothers and sisters, when troubles of any kind come your way, consider it an opportunity for great joy. For you know that when your faith is tested, your endurance has a chance to grow. So let it grow, for when your endurance is fully developed, you will be perfect and complete, needing nothing" (Jas. 1:2–4 [New Living Translation]).

Joy in troubles. I call that soaring higher!

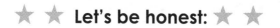

## ★ ★ Let's be honest: ★ ★

*Trials stink. What trials have you experienced lately?*
*What have you learned from them?*
*Do you have joy in the midst of your trials? Why or why not?*

## Soaring Higher in the Unexpected

I sat across from two young faces in front of me. Their eyes were on the table and my Bible was open. We were discussing the story of Jonah, yet my heart was breaking wide open for them.

They unexpectedly lost their earthly father only three days prior.

I shared how God had prepared each step of Jonah's journey. God prepared the storm, the fish, the plant for shade and the strong, hot wind that brought pain. God had thrown Jonah a few curveballs.

Often you hear the expression that "life throws you a curve ball," but the truth is "life" isn't in control, God is. In some instances, God stands on the mound throwing the pitch. In others, He is the catcher calling the pitch. No matter His role—direct or permissive—both are His will.

It's easy to accept God's will when we get good news like a pay raise or promotion, remission of cancer, or a friend who sticks with you during a tough time in your life.

But no one wants to talk about the hard things God brings into our lives. He sent His only Son to die a painful criminal's death when He never did anything wrong. He allowed Job to lose all his material wealth and every one of his children in the same day. Can you imagine having *those* curveballs thrown at you? Probably not, but you may have experienced some of the following:

- The unexpected death of a loved one

- The loss of a job

- A fatal diagnosis

All three hit our church body recently. I can't tell you why God allows the curveballs, but I can tell you that they are no surprise to Him.

### God is never taken by surprise.

Curveballs don't make God swing and miss. God isn't sitting in heaven on His throne saying, "Well, isn't that a bummer. What should I do now?"

•God knew His Son would die.

•God knew Job would lose everything.

•God knew those two children would not see their father alive on earth again.

The hard stuff doesn't make God unloving or uncaring; it makes Him God. He knows what is coming, but He grieves along with us nonetheless. Remember that Jesus wept with those who wept over the death of Lazarus (Jn. 11:35).

Okay, He's God and we're not. Maybe it's easier for Him to cope with the hard things in our lives. But He does not leave us comfortless and He does not allow the curveballs to throw us off our game or make us give up.

God has many reasons for allowing the curveballs. I don't have all the answers, but He does. And from my own experiences with curveballs, I can give you some tips to help you when they come your way.

Here are three ways to deal with the curveballs God sends into your life:

**1. Praise First**

It may seem counterintuitive. You may want to complain. No one would blame you. But, Job praised God when he lost everything.

"Job stood up and tore his robe in grief. Then he shaved his head and fell to the ground to worship. He said, 'I came naked from my mother's womb, and I will be naked when I leave. The Lord gave me what I had, and the Lord has taken it away. Praise the name of the Lord!'" (Job 1:20–21 [New Living Translation]).

Job grieved and then He praised God. Job knew everything and everyone in his life was only on loan from God. They didn't belong to him; he was just a steward. By praising God first, you invoke the very powers of heaven to come to your aid.

By praising God in everything, you recognize that He is still on His throne and in control. Praise Him, not because you feel like it, but because He is worthy of our praise. It is also His will that we give constant thanks, even if we don't like what is happening to us. It isn't a suggestion; it's a command.

"Give thanks in all circumstances; for this is God's will for you in Christ Jesus" (1 Thess 5:18 [New International Version]).

Easier said than done? Try it. It worked for Job.

### 2. Keep the Anchor Rope Tight

When you take a boat out on the water and drop the anchor, you pull the anchor rope tight to keep the boat from drifting. The same is true when the curveballs come your way. The closer you stay to God, the more grounded you will be. Trials have a way of bringing us to our knees, and either turning us toward or away from God.

Those kids who lost their father had a choice on Sunday morning: they could stay home and be mad at God and turn and run away, or they could draw close to their anchor. They chose to tighten the rope. God is the anchor for your soul in the storms of life. A boat without an anchor will be tossed around by every storm and wave.

### 3. Trust His Heart

*You may not understand God's ways, but you can trust His heart.*

God is not out to destroy you or punish you; God is looking to draw you (and others) to Himself. Sometimes that means allowing wonderful things into our lives, and sometimes that means allowing horrible things into our lives.

When God allows bad things into your life, that's not an indicator of His love for you. You can trust God's heart, always. God does not have ill will or malice toward any of His children, only undying love and faithfulness. Abounding grace and mercy.

In those darkest times, when the curveball is flying fast toward you, whisper the words, "I trust you, God." Trust and belief in God's goodness brings strength and tranquility to your heart. When you don't understand what God is doing, trust in Him and you will soar high above the storm.

##  Let's be honest:

*When trials come, is your first response complaining or praise?*
*Do you draw closer to God in your trials,*
*or turn away from Him in anger?*
*Do you trust God's heart when you don't understand His ways?*

# Soaring Higher in Brokenness

I'm not a fan of boxing, but I did watch a match on TV once. Aside from the movie series "Rocky" (which isn't real), the idea of watching two adults repeatedly hit each other until one of them can't get up is not my idea of entertainment. I wince when I see the right hook to the face, or the sock to the abdomen, or the dig into the tender kidneys. I feel their pain and I wish I could make it stop.

I will give them credit for this, though: they never hit someone when they're down. When they strike their opponent to the degree that they can't get off the floor, the boxer with the upper hand steps back and waits.

Our relationship with God is definitely NOT a boxing match. God is not attempting to knock us down or win some kind of cosmic match of life, but circumstances in this world do beat us up. Maybe you are feeling a little bruised and battered today. Maybe you have experienced one of several punches or life storms and you are wondering how much more you can take before you are knocked down and out for the count.

You are wondering why God is allowing all this, why He doesn't make it stop. Take heart, my friend. God is on your side.

This truth from God's Word, and many others, can offer hope:

"He will not crush the weakest reed or put out a flickering candle" (Isa. 42:3 [New Living Translation]).

"He will bring justice to all who have been wronged" (Mt. 12:20 [New Living Translation]).

God sees us when we are down. He is not interested in taking us out of the game or causing us to give up in exasperation. He longs to help us in our weaknesses, to strengthen us during our trials, to empower us when we feel powerless. God isn't looking to hit us when we're down.

## THE BRUISED REED

Reeds are fragile things. We have a few marsh areas on our farm filled with these reeds. They sway and bend at the slightest of breezes. Birds don't perch for long on these unstable resting places. When we feel weak like a reed, God doesn't reach down and snap us in two. He waits for us to come to Him, dependent and calling for His aid.

*Experiencing trials in life does not mean God has abandoned us.*

In fact, quite the opposite is true. God says that He draws near to those with a broken spirit. "The Lord is close to the brokenhearted; he rescues those whose spirits are crushed" (Ps. 34:18 [New Living Translation]).

## THE SMOLDERING WICK

The same holds true for the flickering candle or smoldering wick. God is not looking to snuff out your passion and dreams just because they don't come to pass in your timeframe. He longs to fan the flames in your heart for Him.

We recently had a tree catch fire near our house. It was old and half-hollow from decades of decay. An ember from a burning leaf ignited in the dead cavity of that mighty oak, and we spent the better part of an hour trying to put it out. Every time I thought the fire was out, another spot would smolder, flicker, and burst into a flame. The problem with fire is that the oxygen in our atmosphere fuels it, making it hard to extinguish.

The same is true with that fire in your belly. Even if that dream God put in your heart doesn't seem to be happening in your timeframe, He is not looking to snuff it out. Rather, He seeks to use His Spirit and His presence to fan the flame He put within you.

### God doesn't want you to quit; He wants to prepare you for what's ahead.

God isn't allowing trials in your life so that He can see what you're made of. He already knows what you are made of:

"For he knows how weak we are; he remembers we are only dust" (Ps 103:14 [New Living Translation]).

God knows what you can handle. He also knows what is coming down the road ahead. If you have a dream in your heart, placed there by God, He is getting you ready for it. It may feel like someone just doused your flaming dream with three hundred thousand gallons of ice-cold water, but God makes sure your wick is still smoldering enough for the flame to return and continue burning.

Even if you feel like giving up right now, even if you are certain that the current circumstances of your life are more than you can handle, even if you see no relief coming on the horizon, know this:

**You may feel like giving up,**
**but God hasn't given up on you.**

- God is for you, not against you.
- God is not your opponent in the ring; He is your coach in the corner.
- God may allow things to knock you down, but He will be the One to help you back up.
- God may be silent, but He is never absent.
- God is on your side.
- God can use your brokenness.

Use the winds from the storm you are facing today to soar higher.

##  Let's be honest:

*Are you feeling broken today?*
*Are you feeling crushed by the weight of this life and the circumstances that seem to pummel you at every turn? If so, the Lord is not trying to break you; He is drawing you close to Him.*
*Do you feel like giving up today?*
*Is there a dream in your heart that hasn't come to pass yet? Fan your smol-dering wick and trust in God's timing.*

# Soaring Higher to Conquer

Do you ever watch those epic battles in *Lord of the Rings*, or read about the battles fought in the Old Testament, and think about how cool it would be to fight like that and win over an enemy?

Do you ever picture yourself with a huge sword in hand, charging ahead to fight the foes that oppose you?

I see those battles and read of them and think about how courageous and heroic the warriors are. How strong and unyielding in their conviction to give their lives for what is right and good and true.

In reality, those brave souls had to learn to fight like that. They didn't become warriors overnight. Swinging a sword or shooting an arrow with accuracy takes skill and a lot of practice.

If I walked onto a battlefield with a sword, I wouldn't know the first thing about how to wield it, let alone be able to kill someone with it. I don't have the strength to pull back my son's bow, let alone hit a target with the arrow. You wouldn't want me next to you on a battlefield. I'd be worthless.

But give me a few years to master the art and I would be a force to be reckoned with!

You and I fight battles and storms every day, even in our work. And God can, and wants, to use those battles in your life. It may not look like you're winning the battle at this precise moment, but God is always teaching you how to conquer. Our battles are not won overnight; they are won day by day.

Each time God gives us the power to conquer, He brings us a new battle or storm. A harder one. One that challenges us in different ways than the ones before. Why? He wants us to learn to conquer.

**The storms and battles of life won't get easier,
but you will get stronger.**

God lovingly designed every trial, every storm, and every victory in your life just for you. He wants you to learn to conquer and soar higher. As you learn to conquer, you get stronger and better equipped for whatever is coming next.

## God is making you into a formidable opponent.

He is crafting you into a strong weapon who can fight and win for His team. He wants you to learn to conquer.

David didn't start his battle career with an army; he started alone in a field. He didn't have his first battle when he struck Goliath with a stone from his sling; he had it when he fought a bear and a lion with his bare hands. As David learned to conquer and believe God was the one who helped him conquer, he was able to bravely face the next battle with confidence. David learned to conquer.

Maybe you don't think of yourself as the conquering type. Here's a truth from scripture that says otherwise:

*What, then, shall we say in response to these things? If God is for us, who can be against us? He who did not spare his own Son, but gave him up for us all—how will he not also, along with him, graciously give us all things? Who will bring any charge against those whom God has chosen? It is God who justifies. Who then is the one who condemns? No one. Christ Jesus who died—more than that, who was raised to life—is at the right hand of God and is also interceding for us. Who shall separate us from the love of Christ? Shall trouble or hardship or persecution or famine or nakedness or danger or sword? As it is written: "For your sake we face death all day long; we are considered as sheep to be slaughtered."*

*No, in all these things we are more than conquerors through him who loved us.*

(Rom. 8:31–37 [New International Version])

If you belong to Christ, you are a conqueror by default. It doesn't matter if you feel like one, look like one, or act like one. To God, you are one. In fact, you are more than a conqueror. You are a super conqueror, made to soar higher.

 **Let's be honest:**

*Do you see yourself as a warrior for God?*
*Have your trials become harder? Have you become stronger?*
*Since God is on your side,*
*how does that change your boldness in your current battle?*

# Soaring Higher in Perfect Peace

There is a peace in the storms and battles when we soar ever higher than the storm. Higher because we know the One who controls the storms and calms them.

Remember when Jesus was on the boat with the disciples and a raging storm came upon them? (Mk. 4:35–41). The disciples were freaking out and Jesus was in the back of the boat, sleeping. Why? The storm didn't scare Jesus. Jesus rebuked the wind and waves and everything became calm and peaceful. The Bible doesn't say what happens next, but I imagine Jesus went back to His nap after calming the storm.

The storms you are facing don't scare God; He controls them. He is the peace in the midst of the storm.

**"Sometimes God calms the storm, but sometimes God lets the storm rage and calms His child."**
**—Leslie Gould**

God chooses which one He'll do. Whatever His choice in the storm may be, we can trust He knows best. And in the midst of the storm, if we focus on Him, we can be assured of peace. Perfect peace.

"You will keep in perfect peace all who trust in you, all whose thoughts are fixed on you!" (Isaiah 26:3 [New Living Translation]).

God will keep you in perfect peace as you face the storm as you trust in Him and fix your thoughts, mind, and heart on Him.

God does not want us fretting over what will happen tomorrow or next week. He wants us to focus on now, and on His presence in the now.

### What you focus on
### will determine your level of peace in the storm.

Fretting and worrying over the storm will take your focus off of God and put it on the storm. God promises a peace beyond understanding when we release our storm anxiety to Him in prayer.

"Don't worry about anything; instead, pray about everything. Tell God what you need, and thank him for all he has done. Then you will experience God's peace, which exceeds anything we can understand. His peace will guard your hearts and minds as you live in Christ Jesus" (Phil. 4:6–7 [New Living Translation]).

What a beautiful promise! Not only will we experience unexplainable peace when we hand the storm over to God, but He promises that same peace will guard our hearts and minds. If you recall, that was part of fighting for our freedom.

Peace regardless of circumstances is perfect peace. That is the kind of peace God offers us in the storm—a peace that causes our faith to soar higher than the malevolent weather.

**Let's be honest:**

*Do you have peace in the midst of your storm?*
*How can you fix your thoughts on God in your storm?*
*How can prayer turn your worries into perfect peace?*

# CHAPTER TWELVE

# FINISH SOARING

We are never finished. Our faith journey is an ongoing adventure. In order to soar in faith, we need to accept that we won't be complete until Christ returns or calls us home. Yet, we can continue to push toward the finish line. In order to finish soaring, we must take on God's viewpoint on finishing, instead of our own. To finish soaring, we must have perspective, practice, and perseverance.

When a runner runs a marathon, they have a realistic perspective of what the journey will entail. They know it will take long hours and lots of effort. But they also keep the finish line in mind throughout their training. Then, they practice a lot! They run and run and run some more. They keep putting one foot in front of the other. Finally, they persevere all the way to the finish line on race day. It's grueling work and their commitment is admirable. And though I love to run, I don't have any desire to run a marathon. The thought of running for three, four, or five hours straight makes my quads ache. It's just not my thing.

You know what *is* my thing? My faith marathon with my loving God and Savior. I love this Godventure called my life. I relish my relationship with God, and I love watching God work in and through my life.

**The faith journey of life takes perspective, practice, and perseverance.**

But the finish will be glorious! Better than any marathon medal or record-breaking time. The finish will be worth all the hard work.

It will be worth it all when I look into the eyes of my Jesus. That is my motivation. Is it yours? Are you looking forward to the finish line? Here are a few more things I want to share with you so you can finish soaring and finish well:

# Finishing Well

What matters at the end of the day? At the end of your life?

Finishing well.

Every day there is a path laid before us. There are tasks to do. Goals to meet.

If you are anything like me, you won't accomplish half of them. When I look back at the end of each day and week, I see a path strewn with . . .

. . . moments wasted.

. . . details forgotten.

. . . emails unanswered.

. . . projects waiting.

"I have fought the good fight, I have finished the race, and I have remained faithful" (2 Tim. 4:17 [New Living Translation]).

Finishing well is about getting up every day and continuing to develop a faith that soars, doing the daily things that press onward and upward.

**Finishing well is about continuing on when you want to quit.**

It's about being faithful to the end. Not successful in every task, just faithful. Our faithfulness correlates directly with our dependence on God and His abilities. Not our own. Our faithfulness is the result of staying connected to Christ daily. Jesus Himself told us what that looks like:

"Yes, I am the vine; you are the branches. Those who remain in me, and I in them, will produce much fruit. For apart from me you can do nothing" (Jn. 15:5 [New Living Translation]).

Apart from Jesus and His power, we can't do anything. And we definitely won't be able to persevere and finish well without Him.

It doesn't mean you can't do anything. People all around the world today are going through life and accomplishing much without any thought about God or Jesus. And many of them appear to be doing just fine on their own. But, as believers, we can't do anything worthwhile or of eternal substance, apart from Jesus.

In the verse above, Jesus paints the picture of God as the loving farmer, taking care of His vineyard the way any farmer would. He cuts off the branches that don't produce fruit and prunes the ones that do so they can bear even more fruit.

We have a few apple trees around our farm. We have to occasionally prune those trees if we want them to produce more apples. In all the years of pruning, I have never seen an apple branch we removed from the tree produce any apples. It is impossible for a branch to produce fruit if it isn't connected to the tree.

If you choose to go it alone, thinking you can be fruitful in your work apart from Jesus, then you are like a severed branch, laying in the grass and trying with all your might to grow fruit. There is nothing more frustrating than working hard with no results.

Apart from Jesus, you can do nothing and you won't finish well. Save yourself the frustration; stay connected to the True Vine and finish well.

**Let's be honest:**

*Do you see your life as a Godventure? Why or why not?*
*Do you want to finish well?*
*How do you stay connected to the True Vine?*

# God Finishes What He Starts

God always finishes what He starts. Can you imagine what this world would be like if He didn't?

- The world would only be partially created.

- The death of Jesus would be partially finished.

- The Holy Scriptures would be partially written.

- The resurrection of our Lord would be partially fulfilled.

- The Holy Spirit would be partially given.

- The reality of Christ's return would be partially true.

- The world would be an awful place if God didn't finish what He started. Our faith would be built on nothing, our hope would be insecure.

*"And I am certain that God, who began the good work within you,*
*will continue his work until it is finally finished*
*on the day when Christ Jesus returns"*

(Phil. 1:6 [New Living Translation]).

Just as God finished creation, scripture, prophecy, and all the other things I listed above, God will also finish what He started in you—what He started when you started your journey with this book.

All of us are God's "work in progress"; none of us are finished goods until God says so. That is something we can cling to and know with confidence—that God will continue the good work He started in us until it is complete, whole, and lacking nothing.

Everything God allows and orchestrates in your life has that goal in mind, to finish the good work in you.

When you blow it, mess up, disobey, or feel like a failure, be certain of this: God's not through with you yet.

**If God says He is going to finish something, you can be certain He will.**

God has a plan for you, both internally and externally. God is working in you and through you to accomplish what He envisioned for you before the world began. God has a completed version of you in His plan, and He'll do whatever it takes to make sure it happens just as He planned.

Think of artists who work with clay. Before they throw the clay on the wheel, they already have an idea of the end product's appearance and purpose. It may not look like anything but a lump of clay to us, but as the wheel starts to spin, the artist applies pressure, tools, and water to form that lump of clay into a beautiful, original, functional work of art.

The same is true for you and me. God is forming you into His intended creation. It takes time. It takes pressure. It takes tools. It takes your pliability in His hands.

If we are confident that God finishes what He starts, then we will relax, submit, obey, and willingly allow ourselves to be molded.

 **Let's be honest:**

*Do you feel unfinished? Do you trust God to finish what He started in you?*
*How does being a work-in-progress release you*
*from the pressure to perform perfectly?*
*Are you a willing, pliable lump of clay in the Potter's hands?*

# This Is Only the Beginning

What a journey! What an adventure this has been! Look at all you have accomplished:

- You exposed Wonder Woman, learned why you need to kill her, and discovered how to get it done.

- You were set free to walk in and fight for freedom, as well as lead others to freedom.

- You discovered the keys to win at work by learning about your work: your ministry, mission field, and minefield.

- You learned what it means to have faith that soars and how to soar above the storms of life.

You are amazing! You are now fully equipped and ready to soar! I hope you can see God's truth in yourself now.

I know it hasn't been easy. You've had to face some lies that have been deceiving you for decades. You've had to wrestle with your faith and what you thought you knew to be true. You've had to own up to mistakes you've made along the way.

It is my hope and prayer in writing this for you that you will become a different woman by the end of the book than the one you were before you started. Not different, changed. Not changed, revealed. Revealed, as the woman God made you to be.

Transformed. You might have been a timid, tired caterpillar before you turned the first page, but now you have been transformed into a beautiful, bold, free butterfly. It may sound cliché, but such drastic transformation is nothing short of a miracle. The butterfly reveals what God made it to be. It takes time and a little struggle for a butterfly to become what it's meant to be, but the effort is worth it.

You have sloughed off the old and ushered in the new. I hope you realize what a miraculous accomplishment that is! Take a moment to soak in the victory.

I hope you will use this book as a guide when you need to do some more killing as you fight for your freedom.

I hope you will share it with another woman, so that she may also find freedom.

I hope you will use it as a reference for how to win @ your work and soar in your faith.

I hope it changed your life and will continue to do so.

This may be the end of this book, but it is only the beginning for you.

Go forth, kill, win, and soar!

# ENDNOTES

1 Jill Lepore, "The Surprising Origin Story of Woman Woman," *Smithsonian. com*, October, 2014, http://www.smithsonianmag.com/arts-culture/ origin-story-wonder-woman-180952710/?page=2&no-ist-this.

2 Hillary Rodham Clinton, *Hard Choices*, (New York, NY: Simon and Schuster Paperbacks, 2014).

3 Sheryl Sandberg, *Lean In: Women, Work, and the Will to Lead*, (New York, NY: Alfred A. Knopf, 2013).

4 Nancy Missler, "Faith in the Night Seasons: The Eagle Story," *Koinonia House*, 1999, http://www.khouse.org/articles/1999/234/#resources.

5 John Eldredge, *Waking the Dead: The Glory of a Heart Fully Alive* (Nashville, TN: Thomas Nelson, Inc., 2003).

6 "Women of Working Age," *United States Department of Labor*, last modified 2016, https://www.dol.gov/wb/stats/latest_annual_data.htm.

7 Sandra Crawford Williamson, "Why are Working Women Starting to Unplug from Their Churches?" *Institute for Faith, Work & Economics*, December 5, 2014, https://tifwe.org/ working-women-unplugging-from-church/.

8 Kimberly Morgan and Sally Steenland, "The Challenge of Faith," *The Shriver Report*, September 11, 2009, http://shriverreport.org/ the-challenge-of-faith/.

9 David Kinnaman, "Three Trends on Faith, Work and Calling," *Barna Group*, February 11, 2014, https://www.barna.com/research/three-trends-on-faith-work-and-calling/#.V-Blx_krIqc.

10 Ken Blanchard, Phil Hodges, and Tricia Goyer, *Lead Your Family Like Jesus: Group Experience, Participant's Guide*, (Carol Stream, IL: Tryndale House Publishers, 2014), 13–14.

11 Louann Brizendine, *The Female Brain*, (New York, NY: Harmony Books, 2007).

Join us for a REAL GOOD time at Vino Cappuccino Artisan Bistro!

Enjoy an authentic Wisconsin Experience with award winning local cheese, Wisconsin wines, fresh local produce, farm raised meats, freshly roasted coffee, and home-made desserts.

Whether you choose to find a cozy nook insidethe Farmhouse, watch your pizza sizzling in our wood fired oven, or sip a glass of wine outside in the sunshine, you will be welcomed and made to feel at home!

# REAL FOOD
# REAL FARMERS
# REAL GOOD!

Open seasonally, May through November,
Wednesday - Sunday, Noon to 9pm
Gift boxes available online

## www.vinocappuccinobistro.com

# Coming in Spring 2017

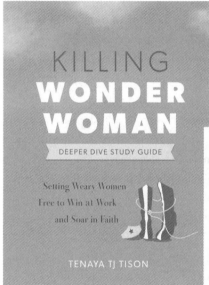

Killing Wonder Woman
Deeper Dive Study Guide

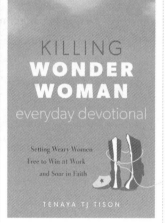

Killing Wonder Woman
Everyday Devotional

# ABOUT THE AUTHOR

T.J. is a business leader and entrepreneur, with a proven track record as a strategic advisor and change agent within the small business sector. T.J. has held twenty-seven different jobs throughout her life and finally found her calling in helping businesses grow.

T.J. and her husband of twenty-five years have two grown children and together enjoy the peace of their Wisconsin hobby farm with a myriad of pet animals. In her spare time (ha ha), T.J. likes to run, play golf, read, and cheer on the Minnesota Vikings.

To learn more about T.J., visit her website: tjtisonpropels.com

T.J. is also the founder and executive director of Working Women of Faith, a nonprofit organization that exists to equip women to win at work and soar in faith.

To learn more about Working Women of Faith, visit: workingwomenoffaith.com

# T.J. SPEAKS

Through her writing, speaking, and mentoring, T.J. guides both men and women to do their work and impact others with purpose, conviction, and integrity.

T.J. provides speaking services to faith groups that propel listeners beyond their comfort zone and into their maximized, full-faith living potential. T.J. helps others look at their life and work through the eyes of God and truth of scripture.

T.J. also provides training and seminars to business organizations to help their employees, leaders, and teams reach their full potential.

This isn't motivational speaking; this is sharing real world experience that forces the listener to make the tough choices and changes that have a lasting impact in their work and life.

To have T.J. speak at your next event, please contact her at: tj@tjtsionpropels.com

**Working Women of Faith**

Working Women of Faith is a non-profit organization that exists to help women of faith grow in grace and in the knowledge of Jesus Christ, to equip them to live out their calling in the workplace to the glory of God.

WWOF recognizes that *ALL* women of faith are working women, whether that work takes place in the home, outside of the home, volunteering, or even in your place of worship.

It doesn't matter what type of work you engage in outside of the home. From Burger King to the Board Room; part-time to full-time; just starting your first job, re-entering the workforce, or working through your retirement years; we are here to provide the guidance and support you need.

Our goal is to provide resources, engaging conversations, biblical guidance in workplace dilemmas, and overall support to the largely over-looked segment of the faith population: The Working Woman.

Our prayer is that you will be encouraged, equipped, and emboldened in the calling God has placed on you to work outside the home!

Visit us at: www.workingwomenoffaith.com